SECRETS OF THE SWORD ALONE

SECRETS OF THE SWORD ALONE

TRAICTE CONTENANT LES SECRETS DU PREMIER LIVRE SUR L'ESPEE SEULE

HENRY DE SAINCT-DIDIER

translated Chris Slee

Secrets of the Sword Alone

Copyright © 2014 Chris Slee (translator)

ISBN: 978-0-646-92636-0 (eBook)

ISBN: 978-0-646-92635-3 (Print)

All Rights Reserved. No part of this publication may be reproduced, stored in a retrieval system, or transmitted, in any form or in any means – by electronic, mechanical, photocopying, recording or otherwise – without prior written permission from the copyright owner(s).

Traicte contenant les Secrets du Premier Livre de l'Espee Seule, Henry de Sainct-Didier. Original text and images are based on the 1907 facsimile edition published by the *Societé du Livre d'Art Ancien et Moderne.* It is asserted this book is in the public domain.

Created at PressBooks.com for LongEdge Press, First edition

To Kathi and Henry,
Charlotte and Marianne

Contents

Foreword ix

Part I. Secrets of the Sword Alone

A Tract Containing ... 3
[Epistle to the King] 5
[Introductory Essay] 7
[Dedicatory Epistles] 15
[The Art of the Sword Alone] 31
[Jeu de Paulme and Swordsmanship] 89
Dear Reader 93
Table of this Tract on the Sword Alone 95
Royal Privilege 103

Part II. Images from the Text

Images from the Dedicatory Poems 107
Images from the Main Text 109

Foreword

The Man

Very little is known about Henry de Sainct-Didier other than that which can be gleaned from the text itself. So, the accuracy of the information and any inferences which may be drawn from it is open to debate. He did, we can be sure, move in elevated social circles.

We know from the text, because he tells us, that he fought in the French wars against the Habsburg dynasty in Piedmont in the 1550s and that he claims to have been a soldier in the service of Charles IX, Francis II and possibly even Henry II during a period of approximately 25 years. He claims to have fenced the king himself (although the Archives of the Maitres d'Armes of Paris state it was the king's brother) as well as such luminaries as the Duc de Guise, champion on French Catholicism and one of the leading figures in provoking the French wars of religion against the Huguenots. One of the dedicatory poems at the beginning of the text suggests that the Sainct-Didier family came from Pertuz (modern Pertuis) in the Vaucluse region of Provence, approximately 30 km north of Aix-en-Provence, and that his father's name may have been Luc.

It may be said of the man that he was from the upper gentry or perhaps the minor rural nobility. He was obvious educated or at least moved in the educated and literary circles of the court, if we may judge from the a quality of those who penned dedications to him in the text: a mathematician, a lawyer and several self-proclaimed "gentlemen." He had an acquaintance in the King's Secretary, Amadis Jamin, one of the founders of the first and ill-fated Academy of Music and Poetry granted its license by the king in 1570. Another luminary to write a dedication is Francois de Belleforest, one of the most prolific authors of the period who translated many classical Latin texts and works of the Italian Renaissance into French and who is credited with writing the first French novel. One of his translations may even have provided the basis for Shakespeare's Hamlet.

With such luminaries writing dedications to Sainct-Didier and for his book, it is surprising that more is not known of him and that none of the French fencers who wrote treatises after him use the terms he appears to have invented. He certainly seems to have had the political contacts to have achieved a more central position within the history of fencing in France.

The Text

There are several copies of the text extant, one in the Bibliotheque Nationale de France, another in the Archives of Blois, and two in collections in the United Kingdom. The text used here is from the facsimile edition published in 1907 by the now defunct *Societé du Livre d'Art Ancien et Moderne*, Paris. The illustrations are reproduced from the same source.

A key difference between this treatise and others of the period is that Sainct-Didier does not describe how to beat an opponent in a duel or other fight but shows instead how one should train for swordsmanship. His text outlines the training of a student (the Provost) by an instructor (the Lieutenant). Sainct-Didier explicitly asks the reader to keep in mind three persons when reading the text, the Lieutenant trainer, the Provost student and the author himself. The techniques and exercises depicted are by their nature consensual rather than antagonistic and often end with one participant merely threatening the other with a thrust rather than actually performing the action.

This, combined with the inordinate amount of space devoted to how best to unsheathe the sword from a quite formal standing position and the essay comparing swordsmanship and tennis, suggests that the text is intended for a civilian and courtly audience rather than for, say, soldiers.

The illustrations are rather amateurish compared to those found in other period treatises and Sainct-Didier points out several occasions on which the illustration has made a mistake or misrepresented the action of the text. It may be that this is all Sainct-Didier could afford; he is at pains to make known that he has paid for the production of the treatise from his own pocket and is now impoverished.

Translation

Translating Sainct-Didier's prose is a task in itself. His language is convoluted and often torturous to disentangle with phrases intermingled and intertwined in the most unnatural manner. Whether this is because he is, as he proudly and frequently proclaims, not French but Provençal in origin or because he is a simple soldier of rural gentry stock attempting to write for the court cannot be easily determined.

The translation is literal where possible. Some liberties have been taken with tense, word order and sentence construction where a literal translation would be sufficiently unclear as to obscure the meaning of the text. These are generally footnoted.

The diction has been simplified to remove extraneous demonstratives which serve no purpose other than making the text sound more sophisticated than it is. The resulting text is more easily understood without losing the flavour of prose. For example,

> ... *having thrown a* maindroit *on the arm of the said Lieutenant, as is shown here-above in the illustration noted by the number of the said Lieutenant, 15, and to the said Provost who executes the said* maindroit, *noted by the number 16, the said Provost being on the right foot* ... (see the text accompanying images 17/18)

has been rendered as,

> ... *having thrown a* maindroit *on the Lieutenant's arm, as is shown in the illustrated noted number 15, and to the Provost, who executes the* maindroit *noted with number 16, being on the right foot* ...

Some pronouns, while plain and evident in the original, have been replaced with the persons to whom they refer where this has removed the possibility of confusion.

The dedicatory poetry found towards the beginning of the text has been translated for sense without any regard for maintaining the original meter.

The names of the two key strikes have been left untranslated, partly because they are immediately recognizable to the period fencer and partly because the meaning of the translated text is clearer using them.

Maindroit

This is the term for any edge strike made from the right hand side, as the term itself suggests given its literal translation of "the right hand," with the palm upwards similar to the Italian fourth hand position, It is synonymous with the forehand shot played in tennis and is called out as such in the essay comparing tennis to swordsmanship.

Renvers

This is the term for any edge strike made from the left hand side with the palm downwards similar to the Italian second hand position. The term translates literally as "reverse," signifying a return or action in the opposite direction. It is used interchangeably with the tennis term for the backhand, "*arriere-main,*" throughout the text. Again, this linkage is made explicit in the essay comparing the two activities.

Both these terms are used occasionally to refer to the right and left sides of the body as well as being the names of particular strikes. In these cases, the terms have been translated.

In addition to these, a number of individual words pose particular difficulties for the translator.

Desrober

It is very difficult to understand what Sainct-Didier is trying to say with this word. Period dictionaries and modern glossaries of Middle French give the word to mean "to steal, to pilfer" as well as "to secretly withdraw," "to take by surprise," "to act in a furtive manner or in the manner of a thief." In the modern French, it carries on top of these meanings the sense of collapsing or giving way (eg: "the ground gave way beneath my feet") and slipping out of someone's grasp. This suggests an echo in the *cade sub gladium quoque scutum* ("fall under the sword and shield") of the Tower Fechtbuch (I.33)

Understanding *desrober* and what Sainct-Didier may mean by it is one of the keys which will unlock for the interpreter the combatants' actions on the sword. I've translated *desrober* as steal as it carries in English the range of senses it seems to want to carry in Sainct-Didier's French.

Jarret

This is a term more usually applied to livestock as far as can be determined. When applied to a person, various dictionaries of Middle French define *jarret* as "the part of the lower limb behind the knee." This does not seem a useful definition as next to impossible to strike the rear side of an opponent one is facing directly. Another definition comes from Cotgrave who translates the term into seventeenth century English as "the hough, or hams," giving us a more useful definition of the hamstrings. Context suggests that the target area specified as *le jarret* by Sainct-Didier is the opponent's thigh. One must ask why he did not use the more usual word for thigh, such as *la cuisse*, for example. It has been translated here as knee for convenience.

Interpretation

Although this is a translation and not an interpretation of Sainct-Didier's fighting style, it is worth highlighting some issues with which any interpretation must contend.

One issue is determining exactly what Sainct-Didier means by *desrober*. The term is used to define these actions:

- passing the point of one's sword underneath the guard of the opponent's sword in a manner reminiscent of the Italian *cavazione*;
- otherwise changing blade orientation from being on the outside (or inside) of the opponent's sword to the inside (or outside) of the sword;
- passing the guard of the sword underneath the sword of the opponent.

The key difficulty is that this action of *desrobement* prepares one to make a cutting strike to the opposite side. For example, one crosses the opponent's *maindroit* on the inside and, having blocked the attack, performs a *desrobement* under the opponent's sword. The immediate next action is to cut a *renvers* to the opponent's right side. If *desrober* referred to the equivalent of an Italian *cavazione*, this hardly seems bio-mechanically possible.

Another issue is reconciling Sainct-Didier's insistence on single time responses (defending and counter-attacking in the same action) as the signifier of mastery of swordsmanship with the double time (I defend then I counter-attack) nature of the lessons he presents. Is this difficulty resolved by the idea that this text is intended as a training manual for absolute beginners, as evidenced by the amount of text devoted to how to correctly draw the sword and the comparison between swordsmanship and tennis, or is another principle at work here?

Given the emphasis in the text placed on how to properly draw the sword from the scabbard and the insistence that the comparison of swordsmanship and tennis is directed at the "unlearned" and is not intended for the "learned" who already understand swordsmanship, the question of what level of skill or training the author intended the text to transmit must be asked. If the book is intended, as seems likely, for gentlemen of the court learning swordsmanship for the first time, it cannot be expected that the text could make them masters of combat. If, however, it is intended for training soldiers already practised in war and life on the battlefield, what could Sainct-Didier expect them to gain from lessons on drawing the sword and the practice's similarity to royal sports? As always, the intended audience shapes the message being communicated.

It should be remembered that Sainct-Didier does not specify the motion of the sword in the strikes, simply whether they are executed from the right of left side, high or low, or a thrust. He details the guard position from which the action begins and the target area on the opponent aimed for. The means of moving from one to another is left to the combatant. The text suggests that all strikes are downward blows rather than, like the Italian and German treatises of the same period, a combination of downward and upwards (*squalimbro/montante* or *oberhauen/unterhauen*) blows.

Nineteenth century writers on fencing saw similarities between Sainct-Didier's fencing style and the Italian techniques of the same period. This is no longer accepted as being necessarily true. The current view appears to be that while Italian fencing may have form the basis of his techniques, his own theories and extrapolations of it dominate the techniques taught in the treatise. Others have linked him to the Spanish tradition of "common" or vulgar fencing rather than to the Italian. This is a riddle for others to puzzle out.

PART I

Secrets of the Sword Alone

A Tract Containing ...

A tract containing the secrets of the first book on the sword alone, mother of all weapons, which are the sword and dagger, cape, targe, buckler, rondelle, two-handed sword, two swords, with figures having the weapons drawn[1] in order to defend and attack at the same time the strikes that one can throw, both attacking and defending. Very useful and profitable for guiding the nobility and the followers of Mars according to the art, program and practice composed by Henry de Sainct-Didier, Provencal gentleman

Dedicated to the majesty of the very Christian king, Charles IX.

At Paris, printed by Jean Mettayer and Matthurin Challenge and sold in Jean Dalier's shop on the Bridge of St Michael at the sign of the White Rose, 1573 with Royal Privilege.

---

1. lit. the weapons in the fist

[Epistle to the King]

Sire, I will not amuse myself describing to you how many there are for hire who work (as it is said) to help to truly perfect Nature, who have resolved confusion into order and those things which, on the face of them seeming harsh, difficult and unattainable, have been rendered by them simple, approachable and easy to begin, wanting especially (the only difficulty coming from confusion and the disorder of things) among other things those which are proper to making gentlemen sufficiently praiseworthy. Accordingly, I will turn my pen to demonstrate to you that in order to rally a regiment which is in rout and put them again in pristine order, a leader is needed having two very instinctive[1] habits. To learn judgement in order to win the time and place, where and when it is necessary to stop the broken ranks and by a feigned collapse distract[2] the enemy, while the rest of the troops re-assemble and regroup. This judgement cannot be bought. Truly the sense of this cannot be understood without the second point that I say is very necessary in the leader, which is the trial of experience from which this judgement is born.

Sire, for anyone who wants to put an art or doctrine into order or draw it from confusion for fear that otherwise it will be corrupted, it is required that he is provided with judgement, born of experience gained in the exercise of the art. I say this not without cause, for having served by deeds of arms, as often your forefathers as your Majesty, during the space of 25 years in Piedmont and elsewhere, I can justly claim to have used my life in the use of these weapons such that long experience has developed in me some perfection in the art and practice of them. Thus, seeing how confused and with such poor organisation they have been and are demonstrated and practised today by all the world, I have in my head some forms[3] or ideas, following which as examples, believing strongly that order will be not only good but that the art of which it consists will be fully restored and will almost attain its perfection, which I have for long days, my impotence caused as much from extreme poverty (the enemy of good spirits) as from being employed[4] in your service, held hidden and buried among my papers in my office, where after martial labour the Muses have kept and I

---

1. lit: familiar, natural
2. lit: entertain, amuse
3. *patron* = pattern?
4. *empêcher*

hope will keep me company. But now the desire I have of doing you humble and satisfying service, joined to the ardent affection which all my life I have had for weapons, for those who love them, and those who make their living with them, having only allowed this time when Mars gives us some respite, I am not bold enough to present to your majesty something not dignified for so grand a monarch but very proper for the practice of a common father to know, as much in war as in peacetime, a tract on the sword alone, mother of all arms, that I have composed according to my humble opinion, in which is contained six points, hereafter declared, in a program never before used and the proofs thereof, both by theory and by the outcome achieved in the end.

Behold, Sire, that which will contain at present these little efforts, which is a summary or outline of the first book that I still have before me. Because if this is to your majesty's taste,[5] God giving me the grace to live, I hope by means of your majesty to put this into the light for others who (first and foremost for instructing the nobility) I thought worthy of you, who are the protector and supporter of the arms of which it treats, beseeching you most humbly whenever[6] otherwise it may be esteemed to please you to take my ardent affection, which has for a long time been dedicated to offering you very humble and agreeable service, in payment employing me with something related to this, and I will hold myself most happy with perpetual opportunity and greatest desire to pray the sovereign lord of the universe to give a very long and very happy life to you and to the limits of your empire, the encompassing Ocean.[7]

Your very humble and obedient servant,

Henri de Sainct-Didier, Provencal gentleman

---

5. *si vostre maiesté prent quelque goust à cestuy cy*
6. *la et quand*
7. *la seule Mer Oceane* - in the Greek world view

[Introductory Essay]

Here follows the secrets of the sword alone and of all the other arms which depend upon it, which to understand, and above all to better execute, six points are required.

The first is how many stances there are in all the art of arms and to select the best and give the explanation for it.

The second, how many guards and positions there are with the weapons and how to select the best and for what reason.

The third, with how many strikes can the enemy aggressor attack the defender and give the explanations for them.

The fourth, to how many targets[1] on the person can the strikes be applied, both in attack and defence.

The fifth, for all those who make or will make hereafter a living of demonstrating swordplay, to know how to defend oneself or to attack in a single tempo whatever strike or strikes one can throw. Thus, if they do not know, how they can show it to their pupils?

In the sixth point, which is the last, one will see a great secret, which is to determine the strikes that the attacker may make on the defender and explain the reason for it.

Regarding the first point about knowing how many stances there are, I answer that there are only two because we have only two feet.

Some people hold themselves on the right foot, others on the left foot. However, to give a very brief explanation, either one stands on one foot or on the other. But in order to be assured when one needs to draw a sword,[2] it is necessary to know which of the two feet is the best and the most certain and superlative and on which of them, as stated, it is necessary to stand to execute the art.

According to me, I support with experience and evidence that the stance which is done standing on the left foot at first in drawing the sword is the most certain

---

1. lit: appropriate places
2. lit: put the sword in the fist

and best, for both the attacker and the defender. How little our ancient demonstrators stood like this and so standing, whether on the one or on the other, gave very little explanation for it. To this end, I conclude that there are only two stances in all the art to start with.

And in order to follow closely the learned and to imitate them, it is necessary to choose the best of two good choices and of two bad choices to avoid both, if one can do it and if not, to avoid the worst. In doing so, I advise all followers to take the better of the two stances, which is that is maintained on the left foot at first in drawing the sword, performing one of the three draws.

Here follows the declaration and explanation of the six points.

The reason for the first point is that there are only two stances, one being done on the right foot and the other on the left foot. As for me, I say that holding oneself on the left foot is the best because, being there, one has the liberty of taking more time and greater scope for action[3] than on the stance of the right foot and, consequently, of attacking well and defending oneself much better, as will be shown hereafter in the sequence of the strikes. Thus, the reason why the stance that one performs on the left foot is better than that on the right foot.

The second is to know how many guards and positions there are in swordplay. I say that there are three guards and three principal positions.

The first is the low guard, situating the point at the breeches

The second is the middle guard, situating the point of the sword directly at the left eye.

The third is the high guard, situating the point of the sword at the face, coming down from above.

Other demonstrators, when they define the guards, start at the high guard. As for me, I start at the low guard because all things begin at the foundations. For example, learned people do not begin to demonstrate the sciences from the top down, nor do masons when they begin to build a house start with roof-tiles but at the foundations. And for this reason, I start with the low guard.

It is very true about this low guard that it may give rise to two other low guards, one on the right side, the other on the left side. That which is performed on the

---

3. lit: the great race, elsewhere seen as "course precipitee"

right side inherits the nature and properties of its parent and is associated[4] with the right side. That which makes itself on the left side also inherits the nature and being of its parent and is associated with the left side.

These two guards are generated from the low guard. They are often made in order to draw out a strike from the ignorant, which will be a *maindroit* or a high thrust because one cannot do any other strike, and which one can easily parry and counter-attack[5] the attacking enemy who will be confused and will not consider the hazards which can happen, being in these two disguised guards. However, the low guard, their parent, is the most certain. As such, there are three guards, as has been said.

The third point is that it is necessary to know is with how many strikes the attacking enemy can attack the defendant. As for me, I say that the attacker and defender can only attack with three strikes. These are:

- *Maindroit*[6]
- *Renvers*[7]
- Thrust

It is very true that they can be multiplied by the six targets on the human body which must be well guarded. As with any good tennis player, it is necessary that he guard well the spirit[8] so that the ball of the opposing party does not touch it. So, it is necessary that a good swordsman[9] guard well that one of the three strikes does not touch any of the six targets to which the strike can be applied, as has been said, as will be seen hereafter.

It is necessary to note that swordplay and tennis are first cousins and he who knows well how to play tennis will easily and quickly understand swordplay.

The fourth point is that the attacker and defender can only attack with three strikes. Well is it true that they can be multiplied and adapted, as we promised above, in their own six places[10] on the person, whether on the attacker or on the defender and he who knows the means of defending himself from the three

---

4. *participer = tenir de la nature de quelque chose (participer)*
5. *touche*
6. A cutting strike from the right side
7. A cutting strike from the left side
8. *Faut qu'il garde bien L'es, que l'esteu de partie adverse ne le touche*
9. lit: thrower of arms
10. *en six lieux propres*

strikes, which are made here and will be defined hereafter and attacking in the one tempo, as he can, being enumerated, he will know a hundred of them.

Here follows the names of the six targets, where one should and can throw the above mentioned three strikes, namely,

- *Maindroit*
- *Renvers*
- Thrust

The first cut and target is a low *maindroit* to the left knee of the defendant.

The second strike and target is a low *renvers* to the right knee of the defender, if he has the right foot forward and, if he has the left foot forward, it will be to the left knee.

The third target, the *maindroit* is repeated from above on the left side of the defendant.

The fourth target to be enumerated is a high *renvers* on the right shoulder of the defendant.

The fifth target is the left breast to which the attacking Lieutenant will throw a thrust at the Provost, which is the third strike.

The sixth and last target is the right breast of the Provost to which the Lieutenant will throw a thrust, which is the third strike, being repeated like the *maindroit* and *renvers*.

Here ends the six targets which is the end of the fourth point.

The fifth point is that it is necessary to know is how to defend oneself and attack at the same time with the three strikes, to adapt and throw them to the above mentioned targets, both in attacking as in defending, observing well the tempo which is required, of which all will be shown and declared at length here-after in the instruction of this sword alone.

The sixth and last point which should be known is one of the goals of the entire art, which is, to determine which strikes one can throw, both in attacking and in defending, because, in determining the strike easily, one finds its counter; otherwise,[11] one does not. And in order to do this, it is necessary to watch the point of the sword and never lose it from view, and in doing this, one will easily determine the strike, and by determining it, one will find the means of defending oneself and attacking at the same time, as I have promised.

The reason for deciding on one of the strikes is that the exterior, which is the point of the sword, is guided and directed by the interior, which is the will, and the point of the sword, which is the exterior, cannot know to be so useful that the eyes[12] and by consequence the sight judges the strike to gain the tempo. The view and the tempo gained can come after or go before the exterior, which one of the strikes which the Lieutenant can throw at the defending Provost, and by that one can find its counter.

Here is the end and explanation of the sixth and last point which is necessary for all to know in order to understand these arms and all others which are part of the same subject.

Following the above-mentioned six points, one named Fabrice and Jules came one time to see me with several others of their country because they wanted to speak with me, someone having told them that I had composed a book on swordplay and that I had dedicated it to the king. They, greedy and desiring to know yet more of the above weapons, of which they know nothing, begged me to show them the book and I refused them (until your majesty had seen it). Then, seeing their true intentions, that they had not come to me to talk but to try to see the contents of the book, it prompted me to discuss with them some points pertaining to swordplay and I asked them some questions, as one can see hereafter with their responses by which one can easily judge who comes closer the goal of the true definition and demonstration of swordplay.

And then I attacked firstly Fabrice and said to him, "Mr Fabrice, before bouting[13] with you now with any of the said weapons, I want to know with how many strikes the attacking enemy can attack the defendant." Then, begging your grace, he told me. And then Fabrice responded and named several strikes, Neapolitan strikes, that is as much to say French strikes. And yet the author understood the response proffered by Fabrice to be "unlimited and unknowable."[14] Fabrice answering again saying, "Sir, why say you that my response is irrelevant?"

---

11. ie: not determining the strike easily
12. *veuë*
13. *tirer à present*
14. There appears to be a section of dialogue missing here

Sainct-Didier answered and said that any response of "unlimited" has no certainty. To this end, the answer by which Fabrice has responded of "many strikes" is irrelevant.

And then Fabrice, seeing that I shook my head, signifying by this that he had not responded to me adequately, gathered his thoughts a little and made another response saying that with five strikes the attacking enemy can attack the defendant. Then I said to him, "Define them," and this time he said:

- *Mandritto*[15]
- *Riverso*
- *Fendente*
- *Stoccata*
- *Imbroccata*

And hearing this response proffered by Fabrice, when he named the five strikes above.

Then the author with very little pause responded to him and said "Such answers contain two items with which you have answered badly because there is one response which is plural and another which is single.[16] The plural is worthless. The explanation is given below. The singular, which, when he mentioned above the five strikes, is relevant enough. The explanation is because there are too many of them and thus it is necessary to remove some.

Fabrice, seeing that I said it is necessary to remove several blows from the strikes, replied to me in order to know of me the true definition and secret: "Tell me, Mr Sainct-Didier, why you say that the responses I gave before, 'many' and 'five strikes', are not well answered by me?"

Answering again the author said "Truly such answers are worth nothing, at least the plural is, as has been defined above and will be shown hereafter by example."

"If one could talk to and question a camp master and ask him by how many entrances the enemy could come into the camp and if he answers by several, I say that such an answer will be uncertain and by consequence not useful, because when one asks this question to a camp master or to another, one must

---

15. *The equivalent Italian fencing terms.*
16. Plural (*la plurielle*) refers to the answer "many strikes"; singular (*la singuliere*) refers to the list of five strikes.

be certain of the answers. Otherwise they are not worthy to act as either the governor of a camp or of a republic, because it is necessary to be certain by how many entrances the enemy could come into the camp, so that one must put on them sufficient sentinels for the preservation and guarding of those within."

"And in order to answer and conclude that which is discussed above, we have equal need to know by how many strikes the enemy can attack us in order to know how to counter them and to defend our body and honour, as does a camp master who has a camp of 100 or 50,000 men – because it is in our particular interest. As for me, I say, along with the learned, that those who can make do with little are better than those who manage a lot.

To this end, I will remove two from the five strikes held by Fabrice because I say they are superfluous. These are the *fendente* and *imbroccata* and there will remain only three which are defined by me above and hereafter.

Hereafter follows the explanation and justification why the author removes the fendente *against the opinion of Fabrice and Jules and several others, nonetheless putting the strikes in order*[17] *for all time.*

The reason why I remove the *fendente* is because it cannot be done properly because, with all *fendente* which are properly done, it is necessary to hold to and not leave the summit and centreline of the thing that one wants to split.

Yet it is that I know no man, as much as he may be exercised in all sciences or arts, that having in his hand a sword, cutlass or other arms appropriate for cleaving, but any strike he may do adheres to one side or the other, leaving the middle. And further, if such a strike adheres to the right side it is not a *fendente* but a *maindroit* and if it holds more to the left side it is also not a *fendente* but will be a *renvers*. Thus, the explanation why the *fendente* is removed by the author from the number of the five strikes held by Fabrice. There remains only four.

Hereafter is also explained why the author removes the imbroccata *from the number of the five strikes.*

The reason: because *verjus verd, et verd verjus*[18] is only one thing, the *stoccata* and *imbroccata* are also one. Because in performing one or the other, it will never be performed the same way twice.[19] Also the *stoccata* and the *imbroccata* are the

17. Needless repetition "have put them and is putting them in order"
18. Given as an expression meaning "six of one, half a dozen of the other" or similar

same thing because it is always the point which does the deed. And by thus removing, as has been said, the *fendente* and the *imbroccata*, there remain only the three strikes which are declared above in the third point.

Here ends all that which is required and necessary to know and to understand by everyone who wants to be skilful in swordplay.

In order to well understand the weapons and discourse on the art, order and practice of them, it is necessary to imagine three people. The first is the author, the second is the Lieutenant, and the third is the Provost.

By the author will be described here after all the commands in the art of the sword alone which the Lieutenant and Provost must obey, which follows hereafter and begins herein.

The End

---

19. lit: one will no longer ever carry to you the same

[Dedicatory Epistles]

To the King by Estienne of La Guette, Gentleman

Sire, it is certain that men were made
And created from Nature unknowing imperfects,
Gross of understanding and earthly of essence,
And that at first they had no knowledge,
As we today, of so many marvellous arts
Used in the world. Rather, heavy and sleepy,
And motivated only by natural instinct,
The barbarians did not care about food
For them or their children, having no other homes
Than the grassy fields, according to[1] the seasons:
Now the trail camps[2] of tranquil places,[3] now
The shelter of sparse oaks not yet intertwined.[4]
Into action, this spirit, this essence of fire
Which lies above the head. And so time gradually
Shined through their closed eyelids,
Firstly to make them admire many things
In the earth and the sky and think more closely
Of their advantages,[5] raising their certainty[6] of
I know not what desire, I know not what envy,
Of changing their ways and leading another life.
So, awakened in spirit and more active in the end,
He planted the vine, and harvested wine
He seeded the fields, he dug down in earth
And forcibly pulled out the metal and stone
From which he banked the walls and built houses.
He subdued the animals and in the soft fleeces
Of goats he dressed. From long, inflexible iron
He made and refined for himself a frightening sword.

1. *ou selon*
2. *les fraix sejour*
3. *des autres cois*
4. *souldre*
5. *commoditez*
6. *expres*

And thrusting it again I do not know how high,
He wings his spirits and flies at full leap
Even to the highest heaven, being prepared,
In the course of the sun, the course of years,
Of centuries, of days carefully he searched for it,
The treasure of science hidden to men.
Yet, my King, the most grand who reigns under the poles,
I do not know what aspect of malevolent signs,
I do not know what misfortune, what disastrous star,
Crossed the Gauls with this unfortunate fate
And made so many minds dull[7] in your France,
Sleeping and veiled in a foolish ignorance
So one find little in them which feels
A desire above the loathsome[8] disdain
Of vulgar ignorance, unsophisticated opinions,[9]
To undertake boldly something higher
And worthy of her name. Yet since Francis,
Your generous grandfather, father of the arts, rather
Of swordsmanship and the arts, and Henry your father,
That valiant noble, and Francis your brother,
And you my Prince and King, whose illustrious grandeur
Cause and promise in France still more happiness,
And your brothers also, these grand princes born
During this common misfortune that you conquer
By your perfections, having the gifts of the heavens,
All the best in you and as demigods
Turning away the influence of malevolent stars
Which the high heavens produce in abundance,
No more do heavy spirits ravage the imperfect
But noble, and happy, alive, divine, and perfect
Because you have power to command the signs.
Yet like a living model of the many renowned kings
Imprinting their portraits in wax (seals),
So the divine model of your mind is made
And formed in the heavens, so many spirits imprinted
With the portrait of virtue and the sublime mark

7. *n'aguere*
8. abhorrant
9. *l'opinion peu caulte*

Of your natural fortunes, as guardians of heaven's
Inviolable law of bettering the best,
Our minds, ever inclined to base things,
Follow closer the perfection of your graces.
For if, as it appears, in France we no longer see
So many heavy, cumbersome and reclusive minds,
Without common feeling, but rather by experiments
They[10] know the secrets of a thousand arts and sciences
No longer are as effective[11] as once so evident.
From ignorance and stupidity to the Arabs, Romans,
Egyptians and Greeks, and now more than ever
The honour and virtue in whatever way
It flourishes is esteemed. This, my king, my lord;
This, the felicity; this, the divine happiness,
You and your race, happy influences.
And from fatal virtue, have in your birth
Sent from heaven to earth, or between both of those,
That in your famous names, the favourable Heavens
Sent down in order to make the homeland
Understand industry through the many invented arts
And the great vivacity of their divine spirit.
Sire, Sainct-Didier alone carries the prize,
Surpassing in honour, in virtue and in glory
All and as many inventors that one remembers,
More so since his fine art was never previously known.
He is much more excellent than others are.
By arms the grandeur of kings is maintained,
Honours defended, ladies protected.
By weapons one acquires, one keeps freedom.
By arms everyone lives in peace and surety.
By arms everywhere we see crime punished.
One looks to keep laws and to maintain justice,
And cities and kingdoms to flourish, being
Necessary for everything to everyone at all times.
But this Sainct-Didier, my good King and Prince,
Is alone and the first, who in your province,
Truly of all the world, was from the god Mars

10. ed: the minds?
11. *ne ceddans plus d'effaict*

Pleased to the Heavens to learn his arts,
The handling of the sword and skill with weapons
Which made the gendarmes so feared in combat,
In order to communicate it first to you,
To whom such virtues are solely an ornament
Then, if permitted by your sacred Highness,
To each your subjects who have been so ignorant,
Unknowing until now truly they have been,
Except for the best advice of your Majesty.
Of arms, the beautiful art, yet no such practice,
Such order, such progress, nor such theory,
(In order to both defend and attack in one tempo
The superb aggressor who will come to strike[12]
Furiously on us) was ever heard of
As Sainct-Didier, Sire, the claimant,
Shows in this book nor was deed ever so great.
The unknown secret of weapons he understands,
Setting down by the art, not like so many ignoramuses,
A bunch of ignorant and barbarous monsters,
Have treated the subject thus far (who show only
To parry vain strikes or foolishly beat away
Without art the adversary with a probing strike
Attacking us, leaving him open)[13]
With one false doctrine abusing those
Who desire to learn and run after them.
And in fact, my great King, one doesn't see many men
Many ready, brave and skilful gentlemen
Who will for a long time teach any crowd
Something notable and the shadow of the beautiful strikes
For meeting a blockhead who leaps out too quickly
From old Machus[14] beaten, hurling them down into the ground.
Standing thus, a man of high heart
Shamefully defeated by a simple rustic
Lacking experience, my young King,
Of the gracious secrets of the beautiful science
That as a prophet flying between gods

12. *lancer*
13. *luy donnast ouverture*
14. the priest whose ear Saint Peter cut off in the garden

This Sainct-Didier took from the holy treasury of the heavens.
Not that in exalting him I should want to slander
So many others whom one sees that I dare to speak boldly
That none of them had any dexterity
To perform with the sword a turn of skill.
So, as through the fields the dainty bees,
Pulling I know not what from the little flowers
A liquor that joined to them from Heaven
Forming by rays their sweet delicious honey,
Thus this Sainct-Didier gathering skill[15]
From the tricks of the past, of the exuberance
Of the modern foreigner or nature, has made
With his own knowledge a perfect work
That fatal destiny neither the wind nor the thunderbolt
Nor any similar force could shatter.
If it may be agreeable to your Majesty,
Never so well has a fencer written,[16]
As one must surely join oneself to an enemy,
That no one in all the world could ever attain
This perfection. Sire, it was never
Not so for him alone and because
Your France in good rights can present itself to be
Above all other regions more skilful in swordsmanship
And you, my mighty King, more favoured by god,
The only Prince under whom they have flourished
And from whom they will have better, through your justice.
Maintained by all such a noble exercise,
Certainly happy to see your achieved fortune
Increase itself from the renown, further from this honour.
Be content, therefore, Prince most high, your greatness,
That your humble subject Sainct-Didier presents
To your Majesty and to your high name,
This small gift from a mind that with so much work,
So much care and effort he satisfied
The desire which he had always to please you.
Crafted and finished,[17] he made it perfect for you.

15. *l'adresse*
16. *traicte*
17. *compassé*

And to you, noble of blood, to whom he has no wish
Other than to conserve the good fortune of his prince,
The faithful accompanying him from all over his province,
Praying that he be allowed
This rare treasure to be put into the light
And that done, it instructs them[18] to defend their king
If one day we want it, in unforeseen surprise
When against his enemies no other weapons would do than
The long swords hanging at your side.
However, my great king, I pray you receive
This discourse of my verse that I humbly dedicate to you,
Together this text, a present worthy of you
On the subject it addresses, necessary to all.

Sonnet to the author by Mr Eagle

I see now, Sainct-Didier, the essence to your beautiful book.
It is the desolate heap[19] of defeated knights
From which the flame opens out, of whom the crowned powers[20]
Cause their shame to live forever in our stories.
I see it – I say – now all charmed and all drunk
On the aroma of your name, shining in your virtues,
There, down under the blade in a thousand anguished cries
Pestering Pluto still from his high river.
Pluto – they say this – you know that our death
Does not concern us so much as to see in this life[21]
That has our proud conquerors envying our conquest.
Yet if a Sainct-Didier we had fashioned
We would hold ourselves well sure of breaking their heads
And from conquered passing to conquerors crowned.

Love and Death

Sonnet by Jacques Brocher, Mathematician, of Pertuz in Provence to the author

To him who thundering across the wide countryside
Harvests the enemy lying inverted

---

18. lit: you
19. *amas?*
20. *les forces escus*
21. *bort* - no clear definition found

Like a denuded[22] pine, his sides opened
By iron tempered in the blood in which it bathes itself.
To that one, I say that the fortune of war accompanied
By fire, by steel, by blood makes itself worthy of the verse
The Muse builds for in this world[23]
Having that which honour earns even in death.
He, who by knowing of immortality
Devotes his fame to posterity,
Deserves a beautiful verse to lift him above all other beauty.
What then of Sainct-Didier who through swordsmanship and knowledge
Makes Aquilon see his illustrious name?
Should not everyone excite themselves to praise him?

By Jean Emery, Provencal, from Berre to Henry de Sainct-Didier, Provencal Gentleman, Sonnet

Kind Luc of Pertuz,[24] the honour of Provence,
Who has borne to us the valiant Sainct-Didier
Who deserves to be crowned the eagle
As much for invention as for experience.
Clear has he made for us — so great is his science –
All the most difficult (things) that are in the art and the profession
Of handling the weapons that in the rack
Have wearied of rolling with common ignorance.
Reproaching you, some are dismissive[25] of fencing
So that your sword[26] may be perceived much smaller[27] than its value.
Come, lend homage to the new son of Mars.
Take the bread of truth and light in his book
Which shows a free and open willingness to you
And to all (of his company) good and brave soldiers.

Elegy composed by Pierre du Fief, Poitevin, Lawyer

Although Mars is not ignorant that France

---

22. *esbranché*

23. *univers*

24. Evidence that Luc de Sainct-Didier was Henry's father and that the family came from Pertuis in the Vaucluse region of Provence?

25. *raco* = *re-arcoier?*

26. *flourès* = *floret*; fencing foil?

27. *ben pauc*

Has had a promise from the gods since its first infancy
Of flourishing for all time and carrying in her hand
The happiest sceptre that human eye has seen,
He deplores, however, that in this her fortune
That she, the strong one, has the graces of Heaven,
The sole and true demeanour of all her grandeur
Is that she has done little to achieve this honour
Than nourish those who train the ebullient youth
In weapons well managed, with skill,
Such as is required in order that from first efforts,
To conquer his enemy as though he were a Hector.
He grieves to see such bad governance
Continue, always caused by such great vice
And misfortune, so that we have seen the inexpert overcome
Him who he must, by the sword tamed
Then moved by pity, from such ignorance,
He wanted to withdraw, our royal France,
Making him his son, this second Mars,
So that much better, she could immediately
Recount to him her wrongs, in order to learn the means
For guarding her infants and overtaking her enemy.
Ha! It's you, Sainct-Didier, that the French people
Alone have awaited from the heavens, chosen by a Frenchman
From amongst those who have taken their birth
From this great Jupiter or some other power
For increasing their name, their grandeur, their reputation
Which had been average, by ignorance enclosed.
Ignorance (O sorrow!) such that one could call it
The mother of great evils without saying anything wrong about it,
And it is now that France must drive
Away her tears and embrace gladness
In order to enjoy the time where the sword of the ignorant
Will no longer see blood, neither coloured nor deceived.
Each one will know that you are not mistaken
In your good life and bodily happiness
As all those, whom the vulgar call
Fencers who have caused us such pain
Yet the arms you have, by the favour of the heavens,
Put into such good order that one could not know better,

Then, if from amongst them, someone (a Frenchman) desires
To see the secret depicted, here could he read
How from this name contentment most high to these minds
He has given and that by desire may the mind
Of the good suddenly understand such things,
The author easily will make him learn
Yet I supply to you to advance all your steps
In order to go lie yourself directly between her soft arms
Which to receive you are open all the time.
Take then my counsel and do not refrain,
Having always search for the rarest of virtues,
From this you would do, not to be clothed
In that which you have nonetheless most often dressed
And which you must choose as the most necessary
Considering the time, looking to the circumstances[28]
Which we have today, that from your house
You leave not knowing whether someone intends
Suddenly to attack you or set ambushes –
In short, he is uneasy that he can defend himself
Without arms always already drawn[29]
Even if there be nothing there but smoke.
With a false report or ill-founded complaint
For starting a fight, a yokel lies
In order to make you feel swiftly enough a mortal blow.
But knowing how to skilfully handle weapons
You can escape all such alarms,
You stand a conqueror, you chase away danger,
Seeing it you can revenge yourself on enemies,
Opposing the ignorant for the least of insults.
Should you ignore[30] or punish harshly
The one who would affront you or another, laughing and mocking,
Without dealing with both?[31] You should attack
The one giving his opinion about another in the mouth
Otherwise one such as him will be a real strain.
One will think in his heart, another will say aloud

28. lit: season
29. lit: without always weapons held in the fist
30. *porter* = wear?
31. *sans que des deux le seul* = cannot make sense of this but in context seems to say this

That this one is a coward and that one a great oaf.
Some other will happen to play the same role,
Again he will say to you, with most angry words,
Alas! Where is the heart who loves better to die
Than to see his honour before him so suffer?
Then it suits you, now knowing
How to be happy, having so good a master
Who teaches you very methodically
How you can live in all places securely.

The end

Sonnet by Pierre Quinefaut, Poitevin

To him who would have them prepare[32] for war,
The sole end of the camp is to train everyone
To know well how he should throw
His enemy coldly to the ground.
To him who in an assault would see the rout,
How should he defend or attack
The enemy in very close pursuit?
Reading this work, he will know the path.
Sainct-Didier, in weapons proved
A noble warrior after finding himself
in hand-to-hand fighting, has described the art of war
In which the valiant and generous soldier
May make a glorious reputation
And be put on the heroic pedestal.[33]

Sonnet

The ardent desire that the miserly merchant
Often displays[34] in his shop
And which he embraces during his day[35]
Because he hates the sharp sting of Mars;
The farmer who one always sees leaning

---

32. *aprest*
33. *parquet*
34. *faict bien souvent estaler*
35. *au cours de sa traffique*

On his rustic plough, hard[36] at work;
And the lawyer subject to his practice;
The work-warrior (mercenary?) known for wickedness.
If only they knew the excellence of swordsmanship,
The honour that is acquired by the arms
From which Bellonne[37] had in great renown and prizes.
If they held the art that Sainct-Didier shows
They may dare to try themselves in meeting
The bravest who may be in this arena.

Sonnet by Estienne de Four to M. Sainct-Didier

To him who goes so high in the heavens,
As to makes his flight disappear to people
And in an art shows himself an excellent master,
Is honoured with gracious laurels.
And Sainct-Didier, who is favoured of the gods,
Opening heaven for us to make known
That which many from antiquity have sought without knowing,
Merits the most grand and precious trophy
Which may be erected to his glory
In the eternal temple of memory.
He, who follows an audacious flight
By his labour with rare[38] noble soldiers,
Has made an art of swordsmanship,[39]
The most ingenious art of all arts.

Sonnet to the Supporters of Mars

If you would know the grace that the heavens
Want for you, chase away all envy[40]
And see here the secret which unveils
The bands which have so entrapped[41] your eyes.
One will no longer judge your art pernicious
As in former times. French youth

---

36. *prompt*
37. Roman goddess of war, wife of Mars
38. *curieux*
39. *de l'espée des armes*
40. *enuie*
41. *estoyent .. detenuz*

Will have minds contented by showing them the skill
Described by Saint Didier, secretary of the gods.
Ever, of honest will, of true heart and good zeal
You must keep this loyal friend.[42]
Practice these instructions[43] and follow his model
For thus you can be acceptable[44] to your lords.
Then, in this regard admired by each,
You will make your flourishing name live forever.

To M. de Sainct-Didier, Gentleman of Provence, by M. de Vaulusien, Sonnet

The Greeks and Romans raised many a pillar,
Many a copper and many a picture of excellent craftsmanship,
And brought to life the painting and the image
Of anyone who invented a very singular art.
You have merited at least the honour, O Sainct-Didier,
For having invented and put to good use
The art that was not an art until this present age,
That under the name of the King you make us publish.
It is the perfection of properly using[45] weapons,
Well suited to all Kings and Princes and gendarmes,
And those out there who profess to honour.
Practice[46] all these strikes, O French nobility.
Have no fear that your enemy may ever hurt you,
Having skill in the hands and boldness in the heart.

Portrait of the King

[Image: Portrait of the King]

Your rare spirit, Sainct-Didier, is discovered for us
In this treatise on the exercise of arms.
And our King, with appropriate confidence[47]
In its favour, gives importance to your work.

---

42. *amy tant fidelle*
43. *escripts*
44. *agreable*
45. *tirer*
46. *immitans*
47. *vertu*

Sonnet to the King

Sire, if the pleasure of your Majesty
Honours this book with even a single stroke of your eyes,
Reading it you will see that there never was
In the light produced a work so valuable.
That is why the favour of powerful and high gods
Wanted the Author, a thing as excellent
As his sweet prince and virtuous lord,
By their commandment to humbly present it to you.
It treats of weapons and of the method[48] and of the laws
That your royal predecessors had never knew.
Thus such a treasure is pleasant knowledge.[49]
Let it take its course everywhere under your strong hand.
You will obtain[50] the benefit and profit which it bears.
It will be for the brave French honour and glory.

Portrait of Henry de Sainct-Didier

[Image: Portrait of Sainct-Didier]

On this page is included the portrait
Of Sainct-Didier, author of this book,
Who has not forgotten a single feature[51] of swordsmanship,[52]
Showing the strength of his daring courage.

Sonnet to the author by Amadis Jamin, Secretary to the King

Justly, Sainct-Didier, does you work direct itself,
Worthy of the god who commands soldiers,
To Charles, our King, more valiant than Mars
Who shames the greatest warriors of former times.
Everything in this beautiful art you want to put to use
To overcome the uncertain hazards of combat.
This Prince, like a god, set all arts
Of nature, knows them and hold them in common.[53]

---

48. *ordre?*
49. lit: memory
50. *ferez*
51. *trait*
52. *armes*
53. *en partage*

Yet you deserve more glory, Sainct-Didier,
Than him who first found weapons,
Especially as knowledge is valued more than ignorance,
And order is valued better than confusion,
And especially that by art and learned experience
You bring doubtful Mars under your control.

To Sir Sainct-Didier, Francois Belleforest, Comingeois.

It is before great kings and their Highness
That martial deeds must be sung.
It is for good soldiers, before Majesties,
That (O Sainct-Didier) your book is intended.
Because swords are of such lowliness[54]
That common people have them, people tamed
By the power of the great may be exercised
In the art that makes them equal[55] to the brave nobility.
This is why it choose you, the King of the Franks
And the one elected of the Sarmatians and distant Poles,
And he who one day will conquer England,
In order that by these three your book may have force.
It also receives from them the praise and honours
When merrily he will[56] lead them across the earth.

To the Same

How would you have benefited (Sainct-Didier) from Bellonne
Hardening your arm under a dusty armour
If your training was barred to the Franks,
So robbing you of the glory and crown
That Mars for your honour and Pallas gives you
For your perfect knowledge? That is why I realise
Your book sings of strikes and full of tempered armour
As a spring field seasoned with flowers,
Because you show how the warrior can
Cover himself and shield himself and how to[57] attack

---

54. *petitesse*
55. *les esgale*
56. *puisse aller*
57. *comme = commë = comment?*

The enemy combatant to ensure his life.
Also it can cause you to be judged a master
Of weapons, an old chief, and very cunning warrior,
Without any other having the means to contradict you.⁵⁸
Bold desire dwells here.

    From Pierre Dufief to M. Sainct-Didier, his Master, Sonnet

As the noble do, I have read of Pompey,
the Roman Anthony and pitiful Caesar.
I thought the strong pack was preferable
If they had but eyes to see so pleasant a trophy.
But such wills have changed themselves a thousand times,
Since I have through you, my dear honourable master,
Seen swordsmanship and seen written the admirable secret.
Yet my soul is more than content on this point:
The Romans have done nothing as easily,
We believe it not so, as you do everything.
Henceforth death and adverse fortune
May come boldly, their ambushes may await me.⁵⁹
Having received more happiness than I could expect,
Their threats do not concern me at all.

---

58. *de t'en porter ennie*
59. *me tendre*

[The Art of the Sword Alone]

It follows hereafter how one should position oneself for drawing the sword, both in times of peace and in times of war, with the steps, guards, draws and postures required by this art, very necessary for those who want to work with arms.

Here, four footprints are put and placed below the feet of the Lieutenant and Provost. One is noted with the number 1, another with 2, another with 3 and another with 4 in the manner of a quadrangle. They serve the Lieutenant and Provost and all others showing how one should perform properly and dexterously all steps, draws, guards and postures under arms.

1 2

3 4

The stance and general instruction on performing the first step for the first, second and third draws which it is necessary to know both for the attacking Lieutenant and for the defending Provost, and all others who love arms, carrying a sword at their sides.

[Images 1.2]

Here follows the explanation of this posture and instruction for the Lieutenant.

And in order to perform this the Lieutenant should stand with feet together, placed thus, holding the left foot in a footprint noted nearby with the number one and the right foot in the other footprint, noted closely with the number two, holding the right hand on the hilt of his sword and the left hand on the scabbard of the sword, showing by this that he wants to demonstrate to the Provost how he should stand hereafter as is shown above in the illustration of the Lieutenant noted behind his hat with the number one.

The end of that which must be done at present by the Lieutenant.

The explanation of the instruction and posture of the Provost.

In order to do this, it is required that the Provost stand feet together, holding the left foot in the footprint noted above with the number one and the right foot in another footprint noted with the number two, holding the right hand on the hilt of the sword, and the left hand on the scabbard showing that he is ready to do that which is necessary for this first stance as shown to him by the Lieutenant – that is the first, second and third draws as is shown above in the illustration and figure with the number two.

Thus, the end and explanation of the first instruction for the Provost.

The guard for performing and executing the first stance, the first and second draws for the Lieutenant and Provost.

[Images 3.4]

And in order for this Lieutenant to perform the first draw, he needs to stand with feet together as is shown above in the first illustration noted with the number one and, being there, he should throw the right foot behind onto the footprint noted in the illustration above with the number three, which is for the first stance and, in the same tempo, draw the sword[1] for the first draw, carrying the hilt of the sword as high as the right shoulder, situating the point of the sword directly at the left breast (counting 1),[2] holding the left hand immediately before the face, as is shown above in the illustration of the Lieutenant noted with the number three behind his neck.

Thus the end of the first draw for the Lieutenant.

Here follows the second draw for the Lieutenant.

For the second draw for the Lieutenant, he should be thus placed with feet together, as is shown in the first illustration noted with the number one. And in order to execute the second draw, it needs and is necessary that he hold the right foot a little nearby in the air,[3] removing it from the footprint which is numbered two, carrying the hilt of the sword, drawing it as high as the shoulder, situating it as above, (counting 1) and in an instant pass the sword above the head, strongly extending the arm, pausing the hilt of the sword as high as the

---

1. lit: put the sword in the fist
2. Sainct-Didier appears to be setting the tempo of the exercise by beats or counts. This becomes more evident in the discussion of the more complex third draw.
3. *un peu a quarter en l'air*

right shoulder, situating the point of the sword at the left breast of the Provost, as is noted in the illustration with the number three.

The end of the second draw for the Lieutenant.

Here below is explained the first and second draws for the Provost, in order to know well how to draw the sword, as shown to him by the Lieutenant.

And in order to do it, it is necessary that the Provost remember how he was placed above in his first instruction, noted with the number two, which is with feet together and, standing so, the Provost, in order to do the first draw, should throw the right foot that he had on the footprint noted with the number two behind onto the footprint noted with the number three, which is the sufficient for the first draw, and at the same instant to draw the sword, carrying the hilt of the sword as high as and a little higher than the right shoulder, situating the point of the sword, being in this high guard, directly at the left eye, holding his left hand directly before his left breast in order to turn away[4] the point of the Lieutenant's sword (if circumstance he may want to advance it further) as is shown above in the illustration noted with the number four.

Thus the end of the first draw for the Provost.

Here follows the second draw for this Provost.

And in order to execute properly the second draw, the Provost should stand with feet together as is shown in the illustration noted with the number two and, being there, the Provost should throw his right foot out of the footprint where it was, which is noted with the number two, placing it close by in making the second draw, which is that he should carry the hilt of the sword in medium guard and the point directly at the left breast. And in order to execute this third[5] draw, he should pass the sword above the head, extending strongly the arm which holds it, and carry the hilt of the sword as high and a little higher than the right shoulder, situating at the same time the point of the sword directly at the left eye of the Lieutenant and holding the left hand directly before his left breast as is said above in the first draw and shown in the illustration noted with the number four behind the back.

The end of the first and second draw for the Provost.

4. *détourner*
5. read: second?

34 Secrets of the Sword Alone

After having shown above, being the first instruction for performing the first and second draws for the Lieutenant and Provost, it remains to show the third draw, of which one will see hereafter the guard and posture necessary in order to execute and perform it.

The guard and posture for starting to perform the third draw for the demonstrating Lieutenant to the defending Provost.

[Images 5.6]

This third draw for the Lieutenant is made with feet together, as was said and shown above in the general instruction, holding the left foot on the footprint noted below with the number 1 and the right foot in the footprint which is noted 2. And in order to begin this third draw, the Lieutenant should remove the right foot from the footprint which is noted 2 and carry it before himself in the air, making the first draw now[6] in its place above (counting 1) and, holding still the foot in the air, turning the hilt of the sword, the top of the hand down and the fingers up, situating the point of the sword directly at the belly, holding the left hand behind, as is shown above in the illustration noted with the number five behind the hat.

The end of the start of the third draw for the Lieutenant.

The third draw for the Provost, it starts and is made with the feet together, as is shown above in the instruction for the Provost, noted with the number two, holding the left foot in the footprint noted nearby with the number one, and the right foot in another footprint which is noted two. And in order to start and perform the third draw it is necessary that the Provost put the right foot, which is on the footprint noted two, close by in the air and do the first draw that the Provost did above (counting 1). And in order to complete[7] this draw he should turn the sword hand fingernails up (counting 2), situating the point of the sword directly at the face,[8] holding the left hand as is shown above in the illustration and figure noted with the number six behind the bonnet.

Thus the end of the start of the third draw for the Provost.

---

6. Provencal: *voy*
7. *parachever*
8. *la veuë*

The end of the third draw for the Lieutenant and the Provost which thus depicts and completes it. It remains to declare here below their [the draws] properties and meanings.

[Images 7.8]

To properly complete with grace the third draw for this Lieutenant, he should be like the plan above depicted in which he holds the right foot before [him] in the air, having made the first and second draw, noted with the number five. It is needed that the Lieutenant, to complete this draw, place the right foot which is in the air on the footprint which is noted in this illustration with the number three, turning again[9] the hilt of the sword with the top of the hand up, as did the Lieutenant which is noted number three because the illustrator has made an error in this one here. But this Lieutenant here holds properly his left hand nonetheless, below the elbow of his sword arm as is shown in his illustration noted with the number seven.

The end of the completion of the third draw for the Lieutenant.

And for the completion of the third draw for the Provost, he should come to feint using the same instruction above, noted five in number on the preceding Provost who holds the right foot in the air, holding the hilt of the sword with the top of the hand up. For the completion of this third draw, it is necessary that the following Provost throw his right foot behind [him] that he had in the air, as was said above, and place it on the footprint noted in the illustration with the number three, turning the hand which holds the sword with fingers down, situating the point of the sword directly at the face or the left eye which is better, holding the left hand directly before his shoulder, as is shown above in his illustration noted with the number eight.

Thus the end and completion of the third draw for the Provost.

The general posture for both the attacking Lieutenant and the defending Provost for executing the art, program and practices contained in this sword alone.

[Images 9.10]

In order to demonstrate and explain this general posture for the Lieutenant, it is needed and necessary for all strikes that he is placed thus with feet together or

---

9. *retournant*

close-by, holding the left foot in the footprint marked number 1 and the right foot in the other footprint which is marked number 2, holding the right hand to the guard of the sword and the left hand to the sheath of it, showing the Provost what he must do, as is shown in his illustration marked number 9.

The end of this posture and outline for the Lieutenant.

Here follows the program and posture that the defending Provost should do, being instructed by the Lieutenant.

And in order to do this, the Provost should similarly be placed with feet together, holding the left foot in the footprint marked number 1 and the right foot in the other footprint marked number 2, holding also his sword to his left side, and his right hand open, showing by this sign that he is ready to take the sword and to do that which the Lieutenant will tell him. The Provost also holds his left hand to his side, signifying that he holds it ready and is scarcely far from drawing the sword[10] and doing as the Lieutenant did, marked number 9. And the Provost must do and follow all that is written and drawn here in the illustration and drawing marked number 10.

The end of the posture and outline for the Provost.

The posture and guard for the first strike of this sword alone for the Lieutenant, which is a low *maindroit to the Provost's knee thrown by the Lieutenant and defended by the Provost, as will be seen hereafter in the first strike.*

[Images 11.12]

And in order to do this, being with feet together as is shown above in the illustration of the Lieutenant marked number 9, this Lieutenant will throw the right foot backwards, a little nearby, in drawing his sword and will bear its guard in the same tempo as high as his shoulder, situating the point directly at the Provost's left breast, holding the left hand below the arm as is shown above in the illustration marked number 11 behind the bonnet.

The text for the first guard and posture for the Provost in order to start the program of the sword alone.

And in order to do this, the Provost should be with feet together as is portrayed

---

10. lit: putting the sword to the hand

above, marked number 10. And the Provost, having made one of the three draws (unsheathings), is stood in high guard, having thrown the right foot behind, holding the sword hand a little higher than the right shoulder, situating and facing the point of the sword directly at the chin. And the Provost holds his left hand directly before his breast ready to do that which will be necessary and needed here after, as is shown above in the illustration and drawing of the Provost marked number 12 behind the hat.

The end of the first guard for the Provost.

This guard is nearly the same as the above. There is scarcely any difference and yet it will only serve for doing and executing the first strike of the sword alone for the Lieutenant and Provost.

[Images 13.14]

In order to explain this guard for the Lieutenant, he should be with feet together and throw the right foot behind a little nearby, carrying the guard of the sword as high as the right shoulder, situating the point of the sword directly at the throat. The Lieutenant's guard, above marked number 11, is the same but the orientation is not because (previously) he placed the point of his sword directly at the left breast and this one, as stated, is at the throat. He holds his left hand below the sword arm as is shown above in the illustration marked number 13.

Thus, the explanation of this guard for the Lieutenant.

This Provost, being thus with feet together, threw the right foot behind and is stood on the left foot, having made one of the three draws (unsheathings) and carrying the guard of the sword a little higher than the right shoulder, holding the top of the sword hand upwards and the fingers below, as he must. The Lieutenant does not. Thus we see that the illustrator has made a mistake in all the immediately following Lieutenants because they should have held the fingers of the sword hand downwards but hold them upwards. But the Provost does better than these. And also, he holds his left hand above the left flank as is shown above in the illustration marked number 14.

Thus, the end of this second posture, which only serves as a posture for the defending Provost.

Here follows the first strike of this sword alone for the attacking Lieutenant against the defending Provost.

[Images 15.16]

And in order to do this, the following Lieutenant, having made the step back and one of the three drawing (of the sword), should be stood on the left foot as in the illustration above marked number 13. And in order to do and execute this first strike of the sword alone, the Lieutenant will advance the right foot, being in the guard marked 13, and will throw a low *maindroit* to the Provost's left knee, raising the guard of the sword nearly as high as the left shoulder, lowering well the point of the sword downwards in order to do more perfectly this *maindroit* to the knee, holding the left hand as is shown above in the illustration of the Lieutenant marked number 15.

Thus the end of the first strike of this sword alone for the attacking Lieutenant against the defending Provost.

Hereafter is explained how the Provost has defended his knee and has thrown a maindroit *across the Lieutenant's arm.*

And in order to do this, the Provost, being on the left foot and having made one of the three draws (unsheathings), guards and positions, is stood in the guard marked number 14 above. The Provost, in order to execute correctly, to defend and to attack at the same time this low *maindroit*, throws his left foot backwards and throws a *maindroit* across the Lieutenant's sword arm and not as ignorant instructors do who cross sword against sword when a cut comes low. That is good because one defends oneself by it but this strike is better because, by this, one defends oneself and also one attacks, and for two good reasons, I counsel you to take the better option as this Provost does in executing this strike, holding his left hand as is shown in the illustration marked number 16.

Thus the defence of the low maindroit *to the knee defended by the Provost against the Lieutenant.*

Here follows the first opposition and follow-up of the first strike which is for the attacking Lieutenant and for the defending Provost.

[Images 17.18]

And in order to do this, the Lieutenant is still on the right foot, having thrown the low *maindroit* at the knee and the Provost has thrown at him at the same time a *maindroit* to the sword arm as is noted above for the Lieutenant number 15 and for the Provost 16. This Lieutenant, being still on the right foot and seeing himself hit with a *maindroit* on the sword arm, has immediately raised and carried his sword upwards and thrown a backhand on the side of the Provost's right shoulder, holding the fingernails of the Lieutenant's right hand looking to the left side and holding his left hand directly before his face as is shown here above in the illustration marked number 17 behind his throat.

The end of the first opposition of the first strike of this sword alone for the Lieutenant.

Hereafter will be explained the defence of the first opposition and follow-up for the Provost against the Lieutenant.

And in order to evade and guard himself from this first follow-up, which is a backhand from above, having thrown a *maindroit* on the Lieutenant's arm, as is shown above in his illustration noted with the Lieutenant's number 15 and with the Provost who executes the *maindroit* noted with number 16. The Provost, being on the right foot in order to guard himself and defend against this first opposition, will cross the Lieutenant's sword, strong on weak, threatening a thrust to the Lieutenant's face and will hold the Provost's left hand near his breast as is shown above in his illustration noted with number 18.

The end of the first opposition and follow-up for the Provost, being himself well defended against this, opposing the Lieutenant.

Here follows the second opposition and follow-up for the Lieutenant and Provost from the first strike of this sword alone, which is a maindroit.

[Images 19.20]

And in order to correctly do and complete this second follow-up by the Lieutenant, he should be still on the right foot. Having done the second[11] opposition and follow-up and having seen that the Provost has defended himself, the Lieutenant again for this second follow-up has stolen his sword under the guard of the Provost's sword and has thrown a high *maindroit* at the Provost, holding the top of the sword hand downwards and the fingers upwards and the left hand

11. ed: first?

directly before his face as is shown above in the illustration and figure marked number 19.

The end of the second follow-up from the first strike for the Lieutenant.

Hereafter will be shown how the Provost must defend himself from the second opposition and follow-up thrown by the attacking Lieutenant.

And in order to properly guard himself against it, the Provost must observe the point of the Lieutenant's sword and when it has stolen under the guard of the Provost's sword, as it must in order to throw at him[12] a high *maindroit,* the Provost, not removing himself from the stance of the right foot, as he is, will cross, strong on weak, the *maindroit* that the Lieutenant has thrown him and threaten him with a thrust to the Lieutenant's face, holding his left hand directly to his shoulder as is shown here above in the illustration and figure marked number 20.

Thus the end of this second opposition and follow-up of this first strike for the Provost.

In these two illustrations which follow is shown the guard and posture in order to do the second strike for the Lieutenant and Provost following the program of this sword alone.

[Images 21.22]

In order to do well this guard for the Lieutenant, he should be with feet together, as is said above in the general outline for the Lieutenant that is marked number 9 which is for showing how one should do all the guards which are required for all the above arms. And in order to do this guard here for the Lieutenant, being thus placed as said, it is needed that he throw the right foot backwards a little nearby on the right side and in the same time draw the sword,[13] carrying the guard of the sword a little higher than the right shoulder, which is in high guard, situating the point of the sword directly at the face, holding the left hand above the left thigh as is marked number 21 in the illustration.

The end of this guard for the Lieutenant.

Here follows the text of the guard and posture for the Provost.

---

12. ie: the Provost
13. lit: put the sword into the fist

And in order to do this, the Provost is similarly with feet together as is show above in the illustration marked number 10. It is necessary in order to do correctly this low guard that the Provost throws the right foot behind in drawing (the sword), carrying the guard of the sword on his left flank, situating the point of the sword directly at the Lieutenant's belly,[14] holding also his left hand directly before the left breast as is shown here above in the illustration and figure marked number 22 to the rear of his bonnet.

The end of the guard and posture for the Provost.

Here follows the second strike of this sword alone, following the program, which is a low renvers *to the Provost's right knee thrown by the Lieutenant and properly defended by the Provost.*

[Images 23.24]

And in order to do this, the Lieutenant is on the right foot having made and thrown the first and second opposition. In order to execute and make this second strike, he advances the left foot and throws a backhand to the Provost's right knee, holding the left hand directly before his face as is shown above in his illustration and figure marked number 23.

Thus the end of the second strike for the Lieutenant.

This Lieutenant feigns not knowing the remedy of this *renvers* but he does, as this will show hereafter, because he does not want to defend himself nor do the remedy but show the Provost how he must do it.

Hereafter will be explained the second strike of this sword alone for the Provost which is a renvers *to the elbow of the Lieutenant's sword arm.*

And in order to do this, the Provost, having made the first guard and drawing (of the sword), is on the left foot in order to execute the strike when the Lieutenant advanced the left foot in order to throw at him a low backhand to the knee. The Provost threw the right foot behind and threw a *renvers* on the elbow of the Lieutenant's sword arm and did not go for the sword, as the ignorant do, holding the left hand on the left flank as is shown above in the illustration and figure marked number 24 to the rear of the throat.

---

14. lit: pants

The end of the second strike, which is a renvers *on the elbow of the Lieutenant's sword arm thrown by this Provost.*

Here follows the oppositions and follow-ups and explanations for such for the second strike, which is a low renvers *to the Provost's knee thrown by the Lieutenant.*

[Images 25.26]

And in order to do this, the Lieutenant, being on the left foot, sees himself touched on the elbow of his sword arm as is said in the other above mentioned figures marked with numbers 23 and 24. Immediately this following Lieutenant makes this first opposition or follow-up and has returned[15] a *maindroit* or high thrust, as he can and has done, holding the guard of the sword with the fingertips looking to the left side and holding the left hand directly before his shoulder, as is shown here above in the illustration marked number 25.

Thus the end of the first opposition of the second strike for the Lieutenant.

Hereafter will be shown the explanation of the first opposition or follow-up of the second strike, which is a low *renvers* to the Lieutenant's knee and a *renvers* to the elbow thrown by the Provost marked number 23 above for the Lieutenant and 24 for the Provost. And in order to defend himself from this second opposition or follow-up, which is a *maindroit* or thrust from above thrown by the Lieutenant, it is necessary that the Provost, being in the stance of the left foot, crosses with his sword that of the Lieutenant, strong on weak, and threatens him with a thrust to the Lieutenant's face, holding the guard of the sword with the fingers of the sword hand upwards and the left hand below the elbow of the sword arm as is shown above in the illustration and figure marked number 26.

Thus the end of the first opposition of the second strike for the Provost.

Explanation of the second opposition of the second strike for the Lieutenant and Provost.

[Images 27.28]

And in order to do this, it is necessary and is needed that the Lieutenant above mentioned, being in the stance of the right foot, will steal his sword under the

---

15. *remonté*

guard of the Provost's sword and will throw again a *renvers* or high thrust for the second opposition and follow-up at his choice on the right side, holding the guard of his sword with his fingers looking to the left side and the left hand directly before his face as is shown above in the illustration marked number 27.

The end of the second opposition for the Lieutenant resulting from the second strike.

Explanation of the second opposition for the defending Provost against the Lieutenant.

And in order to do this, it is needed that the Provost be also on the right foot and that he cross and beat away, strong on weak, the attacking Lieutenant's sword, which is the second follow-up, holding downwards the guard of the sword and the ends of the fingers which hold it, and threatening him with a thrust to the left breast as is shown above in the illustration noted with number 28.

Thus, the end of the second opposition for the Provost resulting from the low renvers to the knee by the Lieutenant, defended and thrown on the arm by the Provost, as is shown all throughout in the illustrations above in the strikes.

And if it is that any Lieutenants or Provosts be left-handers, they should observe the same above mentioned stance, guard and postures, if they want to correctly and perfectly demonstrate these weapons.

Here follows the guard and posture of the third strike which is a high maindroit *by the attacking Lieutenant against the defending Provost.*

[Images 29.30]

And in order to do this, it needs that the Lieutenant, having done one of the stances and draws (unsheathings), stand on the left foot in low guard, holding the sword hand with edge downwards and the point situated a little above the Provost's pants. The Lieutenant holds also the left hand directly before his chin as is shown above in the illustration and figure marked number 29 at the rear of the hat.

End of the guard and posture for the Lieutenant.

Here follows the guard and posture of the third strike for the defending Provost.

And in order to do this, the Provost should also be on the left foot having made the said stance and being stood on the left foot in high guard, holding the guard of the sword and the top of the hand which holds it upwards and the sword flat such that a die can stand on it otherwise it would be imperfect, and he should situate the point of the sword directly at the left eye (that is the high guard) and hold also the left hand directly before his belly, as is shown above in the illustration and drawing noted number 30.

Thus the end of the guard and posture for the Provost in order to execute and defend the third strike of this sword alone against the Lieutenant.

The third strike of this sword alone for the Lieutenant and Provost is a high maindroit following the program of the above mentioned specific items.

[Images 31.32]

And in order to do this, the attacking Lieutenant, instructor, as we have said in several places, should be in the left foot stance as was said, as is marked above in the illustration of the Lieutenant, not in this illustration here but in another marked number 29. And for this third strike, which is a high *maindroit* to the Provost's left shoulder, the Lieutenant should advance the right foot and throw a *maindroit* to the defending Provost's left shoulder, holding the top of the sword hand upwards[16] and his left hand directly before his chin as is shown above in the illustration marked number 31.

Hereafter[17] is the explanation and defence of the third strike which is a high maindroit thrown by the attacker and defended by the Provost.

And in order to do this, it needs that the Provost be in the left foot stance, having made one of the three draws (unsheathings) into high guard, such as is represented by the defending Provost marked number 30. And in order for the Provost to execute correctly and to defend this high *maindroit*, the third cut following the program of the true demonstration of this sword alone, the Provost should throw the left foot behind, cross his sword against that of the attacking Lieutenant, strong on weak, that is to say, near the guard of the sword and a little above the middle of the Lieutenant's sword, the fingers upwards, positioning and throwing a thrust directly at the Lieutenant's chin. He holds his left hand directly before his breast as is shown above in the illustration and figure marked number 32.

16. ed: downwards?
17. *si après* = *ci–après*?

The end of the third strike for the Provost.

Here follows the first opposition and follow-up for the Lieutenant and Provost for the third strike of the sword alone.

[Images 33.34]

In order to do well this first opposition and follow-up for the third strike, which is a high *maindroit*, the Lieutenant should be on the right foot having thrown a *maindroit* against the Provost as is marked number 31 in the figure and illustration above. And in the same instant in order to correctly execute and make this first opposition and follow-up the Lieutenant should steal his sword, passing a forehand, underneath the guard of the Provost's sword, holding the fingers of the sword hand facing the left side and the left hand directly before the chin, in order to beat down with this the point of the Provost's sword as is shown above in the figure of the Lieutenant marked number 33.

The end of the opposition and follow-up of the third strike for the Lieutenant.

Here follows the defence of the first opposition and follow-up of the third strike by the Provost against the Lieutenant.

And in order to do this, the following Provost should be on the right foot. And when the Lieutenant will steal and pass his sword underneath that of the Provost in order to throw at him a backhand on the right side of the sword, the Provost, holding firm on the right foot in order to defend this follow-up, will cross with his sword the sword of the attacking Lieutenant, strong on weak, as is defined in several places above in other oppositions and follow-ups, holding the sword hand with the fingers downwards, threatening him with a thrust to the Lieutenant's belly. He holds also his left hand directly before his breast as is shown above in his illustration and figure marked number 34.

The end of this first opposition of the third strike for the Provost.

The second opposition and follow-up of the third strike for the Lieutenant and Provost.

[Images 35.36]

And in order to do correctly this second opposition and follow-up of the third strike for the Lieutenant, it is necessary and required that this current Lieutenant, being on the right foot and the Lieutenant's sword being on the left side[18] in this same right foot stance, will pass and will steal his sword underneath the guard of the Provost's sword and will throw for this second opposition and follow-up a forehand to the Provost's left shoulder, holding the sword hand so the fingers look towards the left side and the left hand directly before the face as is shown above in the illustration marked number 35.

The end of the second opposition and follow-up for the third strike by the Lieutenant.

Hereafter will be shown and explained the second and last opposition and follow-up for the third strike by the Provost.

And in order to do this, the Provost should be in the stance mentioned above, which is on the right foot. For the defence of this opposition or follow-up, it is necessary that the Provost cross near the guard the attacking Lieutenant's sword, a little above the middle of the Lieutenant's sword, which is strong on weak, holding the guard of the sword and the fingers of the sword hand upwards presenting a thrust to the face of the Lieutenant. The Provost holds also his left hand directly before his chest as is shown above in the illustration marked number 36 at the rear of the back.

Thus the end of the second and last opposition of the third strike, which is a maindroit from above for the Lieutenant marked 33[19] and defended by this Provost marked 36.

Here follows the explanation, guard and posture of the fourth strike, which is a high renvers following the program of this sword alone for the Lieutenant and Provost with all that they should do.

[Images 37.38]

And in order to do this, this current Lieutenant, being with feet together, should have made one of the two first draws (unsheathings) mentioned above, and in this one here the Lieutenant has been put on the right foot in order to show the difference between this form and that which is done on the left foot. This Lieutenant holds the guard of his sword above the right hip in low guard situating the point of the sword directly at the hip of the Provost, holding the

---

18. lit: *renvers*
19. ed: 35?

left hand vis-a-vis his chin, as is shown above in the illustration and figure of the Lieutenant marked number 37.

Thus the end of the posture and guard for the attacking Lieutenant which is for starting to throw the fourth strike.

Here follows as well the justification for the illustration. The stance for the defending Provost, which is, after having made one of the three draws (unsheathings), the Provost also is stood in the stance of the right foot in middle guard, holding the guard of the sword to the right as high as the right shoulder, situating the point of the sword to the Lieutenant's left breast, holding his left hand directly before his stomach as is shown above in the illustration marked number 38.

Thus the end of the guard for the Lieutenant for throwing the fourth strike against the Provost.

Hereafter will be shown and explained the fourth strike of this sword alone, which is a high renvers, *being reproduced here by the attacking Lieutenant against the defending Provost.*

[Images 39.40]

And in order to execute it, this Lieutenant, being on the right foot, should advance the left foot and throw a *renvers* to the Provost's right shoulder, having made seemingly to throw at him a thrust at the face, and holding his left hand directly before his chin as is shown above in the illustration marked number 39.

Thus, the end of the fourth strike for the Lieutenant.

Also above is shown the defence of the fourth strike for the defending Provost, which is a high *renvers* thrown by the attacking Lieutenant. And in order to do this, the Provost should be on the right foot in middle guard as is marked above in the illustration and figure number 38. He should throw the right foot behind and cross with his sword on the left side[20] the sword of the Lieutenant, strong on weak, the fourth strike thrown by the Lieutenant, holding the sword hand fingers downwards and by consequence the top of the hand upwards, and threaten a thrust at the Lieutenant, and holding his left hand directly before his

---

20. lit: *renvers*

shoulder as is shown above in the illustration marked number 40 at the rear of the neck.

Thus the end of the fourth strike for the defending Provost.

Here follows the first opposition and follow-up for the fourth strike by the attacking Lieutenant against the defending Provost.

[Images 41.42]

And in order to do this, this current Lieutenant should be and stay in the same stance of the left foot and, in the same instant that he will have thrown the *renvers*, he will steal his sword underneath that of the Provost and will throw for the first opposition a high *maindroit* on the Provost, being as is said on the left foot, holding the fingers of the sword hand upwards and the left hand directly before his breast as is shown above in the illustration and figure marked number 40.

The end of the first opposition for the demonstrating Lieutenant.

Hereafter is shown the defence against the first opposition of the fourth strike for the Provost against the Lieutenant.

And in order to do this, it is necessary and needed that the current Provost be in the stance of the left foot and when the Lieutenant will throw at him a high *maindroit*, for opposition it is needed that the Provost cross and beat down at the same time and without any little interval the Lieutenant's sword, strong on weak, turning the guard of the sword, the fingers of the sword hand, upwards and to threaten a thrust at the throat or at the face of the Lieutenant, holding the left hand directly before his breast as shown here above in the illustration marked number 42.

Thus the defence of the first opposition resulting from the fourth strike for the Provost.

It follows hereafter the second and last opposition of the fourth strike, which is a high renvers, and it will also be now on the left foot for this opposition for the current attacking Lieutenant and defended also by the current Provost.

[Images 43.44]

And in order to do this, this current Lieutenant, without removing himself from the stance, which is on the left foot, in order to correctly execute this second opposition, should steal the sword underneath that of the Provost and throw a high *renvers* as his own strike, holding the top of the sword hand upwards and the left hand directly before his chin, as all is drawn above in the illustration and drawing marked number 43 behind the bonnet.

After having explained the second opposition by the attacking Lieutenant, it remains to treat and explain this second opposition for the defending Provost.

And in order to do this, the Provost should be on the left foot and, at the same time without any little interval after having thrown and defended the first opposition and follow-up, return to cross and beat down this second opposition, which the Lieutenant threw as a high *renvers*, and should also be strong on weak, holding the fingers of the sword hand downwards, and threaten him with a thrust to the throat, holding also the left hand below the elbow of the sword arm, as is shown in the illustration and drawing marked number 44 everything said in this next text.

Thus the end of the defence of the second opposition of the fourth strike for the Provost.

Here follows the posture and guard for the attacking Lieutenant and for the defending Provost in order to execute and throw a thrust from above for the fifth strike.

[Images 45.46]

And in order to do this, this Lieutenant, being with feet together as is said in one of the first diagrams in order to do correctly this first low guard, should throw the right foot behind, drawing the sword and carrying the guard of it directly before the left hip, the edge downwards, situating the point of directly at the pants or nearby, holding also his left hand directly before his breast as is shown above in the following illustration of the Lieutenant marked number 45 at the rear of the top of his collar.

Thus the end of the guard and posture for doing the fifth strike of the sword alone following the program for the Lieutenant.

Hereafter is explained the guard and posture for the following Provost in order to be defended from the thrust fifth strike thrown hereafter by the Lieutenant.

And in order to do this, this Provost, being also with feet together in order to do this above mentioned guard and stance, should throw the right foot behind and make one of the three draws (unsheathings) and carry the guard of the sword a little higher than the right shoulder to be put in high guard, holding the top of the sword hand upwards, situating the point of the sword at the Lieutenant's mouth, holding also his left hand directly before his breast as is shown and can itself be seen above in the illustration marked number 46.

Thus the end of the posture and guard for the following Provost in order to be defended and guarded from the thrust, the fifth strike, that the attacking Lieutenant will throw hereafter.

Here follows the fifth strike, which is a high thrust on the right hand side[21] following the program of this sword alone, by the attacking Lieutenant against the defending Provost.

[Images 47.48]

And in order to do this, this following Lieutenant, being on the left foot as is marked number 45 above in the other illustration, should advance the right foot and should throw a thrust to the left breast of the Provost, turning the guard of the sword with the fingers upwards, and the left hand directly before his face as is shown clearly in the illustration everything which is said in this text marked number 47 behind the top of his head.

Thus the fifth strike of this sword alone thrown by the attacking Lieutenant.

Here follows the defence of the fifth strike, which is a thrust from above, consisting of a high maindroit *by the defending Provost against the attacking Lieutenant.*

And in order to do this, the Provost, being on the right foot, should throw the left foot behind and beat down and cross the sword of the Lieutenant with his own, strong on weak, that is to say, from near the guard to a little higher than the middle towards the point of the (Lieutenant's) sword, threatening a thrust, fingers upwards, to the Lieutenant directly at his face, holding the Provost's left hand directly before his left breast as is shown here above in the illustration and drawing marked with number 48. If the Provost is a left-hander and the right-handed Lieutenant should throw this thrust at him moving the right foot

---

21. lit: *maindroit*

behind and cross the sword of the Lieutenant, strong on weak, as can be seen by example and practice against a left-hander. It is certain that if the Provost is a left-hander, the Lieutenant or any other must adapt himself to the left-handed Provost in the demonstration, that is to say, that he must make himself left-handed and to do the first step being with feet together and throwing the left foot on the footprint marked in the first illustrations, 4, and leave the footprint which is marked 1 empty as can be seen and in its place.

The end and explanation of the fifth strike for the Lieutenant and Provost regardless of whether one or another may be left-handed.

Here follows the first opposition and follow-up for the fifth strike, which is a thrust from above, thrown by the attacking Lieutenant against the defending Provost that is seen here.

[Images 49.50]

And in order to do this, this Lieutenant should be in the stance of the right foot for making this current opposition and follow-up a little time after he has thrown the fifth strike, a thrust on the right side.[22] The Lieutenant has stolen his sword underneath the guard of the sword of the Provost and this current Lieutenant has thrown, for the first opposition and follow-up, another on the left side,[23] which is on the right side of the Provost, holding the left hand directly before the breast as is shown above in the illustration and drawing marked with number 49. And if this Lieutenant is a left-hander, he should throw the strikes completely on the opposite side of that which is being thrown above in relation to the stance of the opposition and follow-up. That is to say, if the Lieutenant would throw a *renvers* being a right-hander, the Provost should, if he be a left-hander, beat it away with a *maindroit* of the left hand.

The end of this opposition for the Lieutenant.

Hereafter will be explained the defence of this first opposition and follow-up of the fifth strike for the Provost against the attacking Lieutenant.

And in order to do this, the Provost is also on the right foot. The Lieutenant will want to steal his sword in order to throw at him this first opposition which is a

---

22. lit: *maindroit*
23. lit: *renvers*

thrust from above to the right side. This Provost, seeing this, being on the right foot, crosses his sword with that of the Lieutenant, strong on weak, holding the left hand directly before his left breast as is shown above in the illustration and drawing marked number 50.

Thus, the end of this opposition for the Provost.

Here follows the second opposition and follow-up of the fifth strike of this sword alone, which is a thrust from above for the attacking Lieutenant and for the defending Provost.

[Images 51.52]

In order to explain and to give to well understand this second opposition and follow-up for the following Lieutenant, he should be on the stance of the right foot, as he was when he threw the thrust, the fifth strike from above, passing his sword by stealing it on a backhand underneath the guard of the Provost's sword and in an instant for this second follow-up the Lieutenant will throw again a thrust or *maindroit* from above, at his choice, on the left side of the defending Provost, holding the top of the sword hand downwards and the fingers upwards and holding the left hand directly before his breast as is shown above in the illustration and drawing marked number 51.

The end of the second opposition for the Lieutenant.

Hereafter is explained the protection and defence of the second opposition of the fifth strike from which one must guard the immediately following Provost against the Lieutenant.

And in order to do this, it is needed that the Provost, being in the stance of the right foot, cross and beat away the sword of the attacking Lieutenant, strong on weak, on a *maindroit* otherwise called a forehand, and by this means the Provost will defend and will evade the second opposition and follow-up thrown above by the Lieutenant and, all that done, the Provost threatens a thrust to the Lieutenant's face, holding the guard of the his sword, the fingers of the sword hand, upwards and the left hand directly before the left breast as is shown here above in the following illustration marked number 52 at the back of his hat.

The end of the second opposition and follow-up of the fifth strike, which is a thrust from above on the right side, defended by the Provost against the demonstrating Lieutenant.

Here is the guard and posture of the Lieutenant and Provost for the thrust, the sixth strike on the defender, being enumerated in its own sixth item.

[Images 53.54]

It is necessary to explain this next guard and posture for making and executing the thrust, the sixth and last strike and item, as was said, being enumerated above in several strikes and oppositions of this sword alone. In this one, it is reproduced on the right side. One could start to throw it on the left side but one should reproduce the strikes or execute them with a feint. But in this guard, in order to start this sixth strike by the Lieutenant, he will throw himself on the right foot in middle guard, holding the top of the sword hand upwards, situating the point of the sword directly at the face of the Provost, and the holding left hand directly before his chin, as is shown in his illustration marked number 53 behind the throat.

It should be noted that the left-hander, in order to defend well this thrust from above, he should hold himself on the left foot and cross the sword from strong to weak in order to defend it, as will be seen hereafter in the strikes which follow.

The end and the explanation of the posture and guard by this Lieutenant.

Here follows the explanation of the guard and posture for the Provost in order to prepare himself to defend the thrust from above, which will be thrown hereafter by the Lieutenant against the Provost, in the sixth and last strike being enumerated, as was said, in the sixth item.

This guard and posture for the Provost is that he should be on the right foot, just as the Lieutenant. Notwithstanding that he could hold himself on the left foot and advance the right foot, in this last strike and item being enumerated we will treat this guard as being done on the right foot. In order to do this, the Provost will be on the right foot in low guard, holding the fingers of the sword hand downwards, situating the point of the sword directly at the belly of the Lieutenant and holding his left hand directly before his breast, as one can see above in the illustration and figure marked number 54 near the feather of his bonnet.

It should be noted that all left-handers who follow this instruction, both for the Lieutenant and the the Provost, the stance to the opposite, the draws (unsheathings) likewise and the strikes also opposite to that of the right-handers and those who follow this reasoning will definitely find the experience good. Thus, the end of the stance and guard for the Provost in order to defend himself from the sixth strike which will here hereafter thrown by the demonstrating Lieutenant.

Thus the end of the posture and guard for the Provost in order to be defended from the sixth strike which will be thrown hereafter by the teaching Lieutenant.

Here follows the sixth and last strike and item of this sword alone being enumerated which is a thrust from above on the left side[24] thrown by the attacking Lieutenant against the defending Provost.

[Images 55.56]

And in order to do this, the following Lieutenant should be in the guard and stance as said above and shown in the illustration marked number 53. This following Lieutenant, being on the right foot as is said, will pretend[25] to throw a thrust to the left side of the Provost on the right foot and in an instant will advance the left foot, stealing his sword underneath the guard of the Provost's sword and will throw at him a thrust to the right side, holding the guard of the sword and the ends of the fingers of the sword hand looking to the left side, and holding his left hand directly before his left breast as is shown in the illustration marked number 55 at the rear of the collar of the Lieutenant.

The end and the explanation of this sixth and last strike of this sword alone for the attacking Lieutenant.

After having treated of the sixth and last strike of this sword alone by the attacking Lieutenant, it remains also to treat of the defence of it by the defending Provost.

And in order to do this, being on the right foot as is shown in the illustration marked number 54 and, being in his guard, the Provost will throw it behind and will cross his sword with that of the attacking Lieutenant, beating away and defending the thrust, strong on weak — explaining again which is the strong and the weak: it is that he should cross all strikes near the guard of the sword against the middle of the enemy's sword and thus the strong on the weak – and, this done, the Provost will threaten a thrust to the chest of the attacking Lieu-

---

24. lit: *renvers*
25. lit: make to seem

tenant, holding the top of the sword hand upwards and the left hand below the elbow of the sword arm as is shown above in the illustration marked number 56.

The end and explanation of the defence of the sixth and last strike for the defending Provost against the attacking Lieutenant.

Here follows the first opposition and follow-up of the sixth and last strike being enumerated which is a thrust from above for the attacking Lieutenant and defended by the Provost that is here.

[Images 57.58]

Here is shown by Henry de Sainct-Didier, the author, what this Lieutenant must do in order to correctly assault the Provost on this last strike and item of this sword alone following the art and the program for it.

And in order to do this, this Lieutenant, being on the left foot, has thrown the sixth strike as is shown above in the illustration marked number 55. His sword being on the backhand and in order to correctly do and execute this first follow-up, this following Lieutenant will steal his sword underneath the guard of the Provost's sword and will throw at him a thrust on the right side[26] for this first opposition, turning the fingers of the sword hand upwards and (holding) his left hand directly before his face in order to avoid the point of the sword of the Provost as is shown above in the illustration and drawing marked number 57 behind the neck of the Lieutenant.

The end of the first opposition and follow-up of the sixth strike and item for the attacking Lieutenant.

Hereafter is the defence of this first opposition and follow-up for the Provost of the sixth strike, which is a thrust from above being as is said reproduced and thrown by the attacking Lieutenant and defended by the Provost, as will be seen by this text here after, in which the author conducts and shows how the Provost must defend himself from this thrust.

And in order to do this, the Provost must stand firm and stable in the stance of the left foot and for the defence and protection from this opposition, which will

26. *maindroit*

be a thrust, the Provost will cross with his sword the sword of the Lieutenant, strong on weak, coming from the right hand side,[27] carrying the fingers of the sword hand upwards, threatening a thrust to the Lieutenant's face. The Provost also holds his left hand directly before his left breast as is shown above in the illustration marked number 58.

Thus the end and defence of the first opposition and follow-up of the sixth and last strike for the defending Provost.

Here is the second and last opposition and follow-up of the sixth strike being enumerated which is a thrust from above on the left side, coming from the thrust on the right side by the Lieutenant against the Provost, which is executed here.

[Images 59.60]

And in order to do this, this following Lieutenant should be on the left foot and his sword in the first opposition, which is on the right-hand side[28] or thrust from there, as is shown in the illustration marked 57. It is needed and necessary in order to execute this second and last opposition for this Lieutenant that he steal his sword underneath the guard of the Provost's sword and throw another thrust on the backhand, holding the top of the sword hand upwards and his left hand directly before his face in order to defend the point of the sword of the Provost, if he pushed it further forward, as is shown above in illustration marked number 59 behind the hat.

Here is the end of the second and last opposition and follow-up by the attacking Lieutenant against the defending Provost.

The defence of this second opposition or follow-up of the sixth and last strike of this sword alone, which is a thrust from above on the left side,[29] for the defending Provost against the attacking Lieutenant.

And for the defence of this second opposition and follow-up for the Provost, he should be on the left foot and, being there, must cross with his sword that of the Lieutenant, strong on weak, which is near the guard against the middle of the Lieutenant's sword as has been said above in several places, and threaten a

---

27. lit: from the side of the *maindroit*
28. lit: *maindroit*
29. *renvers*

thrust at the left breast or to the eye of the Lieutenant, having the fingers of the sword hand downwards and the left hand directly before the belly underneath the elbow of the sword arm as is shown in the illustration marked number 60 behind the hat.

Thus the end of the six strikes being enumerated in their own items, as has been said above, with oppositions and follow-ups, both for the attacking Lieutenant and for the defending Provost.

Here is shown the guard and posture for making two good and subtle strikes in the form of a triangle and a quadrangle for the attacking Lieutenant against the defending Provost.

[Images 61.62]

And in order to do this, this current Lieutenant, having made one of the three draws (unsheathings) with its proper stance,[30] is stood on the left foot which is placed and put[31] on the footprint of the triangle noted with number 1 and is in middle guard, situating the point of the sword directly at the left breast of the Provost, holding the left hand on the left hip, as noted above with number 61 behind the hat in the illustration.

And if he is left-landed, he should hold his right foot on the triangle if he wants to properly execute and make the first strike, as will be shown hereafter, and will hold himself in the same guard if he is attacking as noted with number 61 in this illustration of the right-handed Lieutenant.

Thus the end of the guard and posture for the Lieutenant in order to execute the triangle against the defending Provost.

Here follows the declaration, guard and posture of the triangle for the defending Provost.

And in order to do this, the next Provost should be on the left foot, holding this foot on the corner of the triangle which is noted number 1 in this illustration, having made one of the draws (unsheathings) with its own proper stance and is stood in high guard, holding the top of the sword hand upwards, situat-

---

30. *avec sa desmarche a ce propres*
31. *pausé*

ing the point of the sword directly at the left eye of the Lieutenant and the left hand directly before his breast ready to turn away the point of the sword of the attacking Lieutenant, as is figured above in the illustration noted with number 62.

The end of the guard and stance for the defending Provost.

Here follows what he should do in order to execute a very good and subtle strike against the defending Provost. The attacking Lieutenant imagines a triangle on the ground which they both have under their feet in order to do it well.[32]

[Images 63.64]

And in order to start well, this Lieutenant will advance the right foot, which he holds behind in the illustration noted with number 61, on the footprint near the corner of the triangle noted with number 2, and throws a thrust to the face of the Provost, holding the fingers of the sword hand upwards and the left hand directly before the face, as is shown clearly[33] here in this illustration of the Lieutenant noted with number 63.

Thus, how the Lieutenant, who will serve to show it, must throw a thrust in order to start to do this triangle.

Here follows how the Provost must defend himself from the thrust thrown by the Lieutenant on the figure in the form of a triangle.

And in order to do this,[34] having made the stance, guard and position[35] made in this illustration noted with number 62, this Provost threw the left foot behind and put it on the footprint which is or must be noted with number 2 and this Provost crossed the sword coming in on a thrust thrown by the Lieutenant, the strong on the weak, which is explained in several places, for both the strikes and the oppositions and follow-ups, turning the fingers of the sword hand upwards and threatening a thrust to the face of the Lieutenant, holding the left hand directly before and above the thigh, as is here above in the illustration noted with number 64.

---

32. This paragraph is torturous in the original with two phrases completely intermixed and intertwined.
33. *apertement*
34. repeated subject deleted
35. *assituation*

Thus the end of the first strike and beginning of the defence that the Lieutenant will throw against the Provost.

And for the first opposition and follow-up of the triangle for the attacking Lieutenant against the defending Provost, the Lieutenant makes a thrust or renvers from above.

[Images 65.66]

In order to properly do this first opposition and follow-up, the Lieutenant, who should have the left foot on the footprint of the triangle which is noted in the illustrations with number 1, will advance the right foot onto the footprint which is noted, or should be, with number 3, and pass the point of the sword underneath the guard of the Provost's sword, having made and thrown for this first opposition and follow-up the above-said strike and thrown a thrust from above on the right-hand side of the Provost, holding the fingers of the sword hand downwards and the left hand directly before the breast as is shown in this illustration noted with number 65.

The end of the first opposition and follow-up of the triangle for the attacking Lieutenant against the defending Provost.

Here follows the defence of the first opposition and follow-up for the Provost against the Lieutenant.

And in order to do this, the Provost should watch the point of the Lieutenant's sword. When it passes underneath the guard of his sword in order to throw at him a thrust from above or *renvers*, at the Lieutenant's choice given that he is attacking and for the protection[36] of this first opposition and follow-up of this triangle, made by the Lieutenant, it is required that the Provost cross the Lieutenant's sword, the strong on the weak, and being on the right foot, threaten a thrust to the face of the Lieutenant, holding the top of the sword hand upwards and the left hand directly before the breast as is shown above in the illustration noted with number 66.

Thus the end and defence of the first opposition of the triangle for the Provost.

Here follows the second opposition and follow-up, which is a thrust or maindroit from

---

36. *la conservation*

above, resulting from[37] the strike of the triangle for the attacking Lieutenant against the defending Provost.

[Images 67.68]

And again[38] for this second opposition of the triangle, if the Lieutenant sees that the Provost may be defended from this first opposition, made and thrown on the backhand by the Provost as is noted with number 66 and that he may be skilful,[39] this current Lieutenant, being stood in the same stance of the right foot, will steal his sword underneath the guard of the Provost's sword by a backhand and will pretend[40] to throw a backhand to the thigh of the Provost, lifting in the same instant his sword upwards and in order to execute this second opposition will cross the Provost's sword, strong to weak, and threaten him with a thrust to the body or face, changing the right foot, which is on the corner of the triangle noted with number 3, and putting it on the footprint noted with 2, holding the fingers of the sword hand upwards and the left hand directly before the face as is shown in the illustration noted with number 67 behind the hat.

The the end for the Lieutenant against the Provost.

Here follows the counter for the second opposition and follow-up for the Provost.

And in order to do this, the Provost should be on the left foot having made his stance, as said above in the figures of the three draws (unsheathings) noted with numbers 2 and 4 and as is also shown above in the illustration of the Provost, 62. And in order to properly guard himself from this strike thrown by the Lieutenant, in the form and manner of a triangle, the Provost should watch closely[41] the point of the Lieutenant's sword and never lose it from view and when the Lieutenant advances his right foot in order to throw a thrust or renvers from above, this current Provost should cross these strikes, strong on weak, and threaten him with a thrust to the face, as is shown above in this illustration noted with number 64. And in order to do and execute this second opposition for this Provost, he will be on the right foot and cross the thrust coming on the left side[42] that the Lieutenant will have thrown, strong on weak, holding the fingers of the sword

---

37. *provenant*
38. repeated subject deleted
39. *adroit*
40. *faire semblant*
41. *bien* = well?
42. *renvers*

hand upwards threatening a thrust to the Lieutenant's face and the Provost will hold his left hand directly before his pants as in noted here above with number 68.

Thus the end and defence of the strike for the Provost.

Posture and guard of the first strike in order to execute and make the quadrangle for the Lieutenant and Provost.

[Images 69.70]

It should be well noted that in order to do and execute this quadrangle for the Lieutenant, he should have the left foot on the corner of the quadrangle noted with number 1, having made one of the three draws (unsheathings) with its stance and this guard should be middlingly[43] low, the edge of the sword downwards and the point of the sword directly at the stomach, holding the left hand directly before the belly, as is shown above in the illustration noted with number 69.

The end of the guard and posture for the Lieutenant in order to start, do and execute the quadrangle against the defending Provost.

The definition, guard and posture for the defending Provost in order to guard himself and to defend from the quadrangle thrown by the attacking Lieutenant against the defending Provost.

And in order to do this, the Provost should be on the left foot, of which this foot will be put on the footprint which is noted with number 1 in his quadrangle, being in medium guard having made his stance and drawing (the sword) as said above in several places, holding the guard with the top of the sword hand upwards and by consequence the fingers of this hand downwards and the left hand on his left hip, as is shown above in his illustration and figure noted with number 70.

Hereafter will be shown a very good strike for the attacking Lieutenant and for the defending Provost in the form of a quadrangle and all that which it is required to know by the Lieutenants and Provosts and by consequence all other supporters.[44]

---

43. *moyennement*
44. *suppots* – other members of the salle, perhaps?

The first strike and follow-up of the quadrangle for the Lieutenant and Provost.

[Images 71.72]

And in order to do it well, it is needed for the first strike that the Lieutenant, having made one of the draws (unsheathings), stand on the left foot which is on the footprint noted with number 1. In order to execute this strike, this Lieutenant should advance the right foot on the footprint which is noted with number 2 and throw a quick and strong[45] thrust from above, holding the fingers of the sword hand upwards and the left hand on the right hip as is shown above in his illustration noted with number 71 behind the hat.

Thus how the Lieutenant should start to do this strike in the form of a quadrangle, pretending it thus to be on the ground.[46]

Here follows how the Provost should defend himself from this strike, made and thrown by the Lieutenant, pretending and drawing a quadrangle in the earth, such as this one above.

And in order to do this, the Provost should be on the left foot as is shown and said above in the first posture. And in order to defend this strike properly, made as said in a quadrangle by the Lieutenant on a thrust or *maindroit* from above, the Provost will throw the left foot from the footprint of the quadrangle which is noted 1 and will pause the left foot on a little corner of the triangle which is noted with number 3 and will cross the Lieutenant's sword, strong on weak, turning away the *maindroit* or thrust thrown in a quadrangle by the Lieutenant, as was said, the Provost threatening a thrust directly to the Lieutenant's left eye and holding the fingers of the sword hand upwards and the left hand directly before his pants as is shown above in the illustration of the Provost noted with number 72.

Thus that which the Provost must do in order to defend himself from the quadrangle thrown by the attacking Lieutenant.

The first opposition and follow-up of the quadrangle for the Lieutenant and Provost.

[Images 73.74]

---

45. *roide* carries both meaning strongly
46. la terre

And in order to continue to execute this first opposition or follow-up of the quadrangle for the Lieutenant, it is again needed that he make a follow-up, seeing that the Provost has been skilful and not ignorant, understanding that he has defended himself well. For this reason, the Lieutenant must steal his sword underneath the guard of the Provost's sword and put the left foot on the footprint which is noted with number 3, passing a *maindroit*, throwing the body a little to the rear and raising the right foot from the place where was noted with number 2. Just as it is shown above in his illustration noted with number 73 behind the hat.

Thus that which the Lieutenant must again do for the first opposition as is required for this first strike of the quadrangle.

Here follows the defence of this first opposition and follow-up of this quadrangle for the defending Provost against the attacking Lieutenant.

And in order to do this, the Provost should be on the left foot on the corner of his triangle which is noted with number 1 and the right foot on the footprint which is also noted with number 2. And for the defence of this first follow-up, the Provost, being on the right foot, has crossed the Lieutenant's sword, strong on weak, and threatened him with a thrust to the face, holding the top of the sword hand upwards and holding the left hand directly before the breast as is shown here above in his illustration and figure noted with number 74.

Thus that which the Provost must do in order to guard himself from this opposition which the Lieutenant threw just now.

Here follows the completion of the quadrangle which is a maindroit or thrust from above thrown by the Lieutenant against the Provost.

[Images 75.76]

In order to properly complete this quadrangle for the Lieutenant against the Provost, the Lieutenant should, having the right foot on the footprint noted with number 4 and the left foot on the footprint noted 3, steal his sword underneath the guard of the Provost's sword and throw a *maindroit* or thrust from above in order to complete the quadrangle. The Lieutenant holds the fingers of the sword hand downwards and the left hand before his face as is shown above in his illustration noted with number 75.

Thus the completion of the strike made in the form of the quadrangle for the Lieutenant against the defending Provost.

Here follows the defence and completion of the strike with its two follow-ups in the form of a quadrangle for the defending Provost against the attacking Lieutenant.

And in order to do this, the Provost should for this first[47] follow-up, being on the right foot, cross and beat down the *renvers* or thrust from above thrown on this one by the Lieutenant, strong on weak, holding the guard of the sword with) the fingers of the sword hand downwards, throwing a thrust from above to the left eye of the Lieutenant, as is shown above in this illustration and figure noted with number 74 as with other illustrations. And for this second opposition and follow-up, which is the completion of this quadrangle, the Provost should also be on the right foot and watch carefully the point of the Lieutenant's sword, as in all the discourse of the quadrangle, and cross the Lieutenant's sword making this second opposition, which is a *maindroit* or thrust from above coming from him,[48] strong on weak, holding the fingers of the sword hand upwards threatening the Lieutenant with a thrust to his face, holding the left hand to his breast as is shown above in his illustration noted with number 76.

The end of the quadrangle for the Provost.

After having treated above of all the art, program and practice of the sword alone and defined all which is required for it, both for the attacker and the defender, I really want hereafter to treat and show four very good and subtle holds[49] *which they can do, both for the attacker and the defender, as will be seen hereafter in their illustrations.*

Hereafter is shown and explained the agenda and posture for the attacking Lieutenant in order to show how to perform the first hold against the Provost.

[Images 77.78]

And in order to do this, this next Lieutenant should be on the left foot having made, as was said, his stance, guard and position mentioned above in the first outlines. And for this, he should hold himself on the right foot in middle guard, holding the fingers of the sword hand downwards and the left hand directly

---

47. ed: second?
48. *provenant d'iceluy*
49. prinzes

before the face in order to keep it close[50] to beat away a thrust from above if it happens that the Provost or other defender throws one at him — because all thrusts are easy to defend and to turn aside with the hand and one will not fail since the point is in the air and far from the force from which it proceeds, which is from its thrower. And all things which are in the air are simple to turn aside, as the Lieutenant is ready to do if it happens that the Provost advances his point further, as is shown above in his illustration numbered 77 behind the throat.

The end of the guard and posture for the attacking Lieutenant who wants to show the Provost how to make the first hold.

Here follows the guard and posture for the Provost in order to defend against the Lieutenant's first hold which will be seen hereafter in the illustration which follows marked 90.[51]

And for this guard, it is required that the Provost has made the same stance, guard and position, as was said above in one of the draws (unsheathings), having thrown the right foot behind and being stood on the left foot in high guard, holding the sword hand with the finger downwards, situating the point of it directly at the left eye of the Lieutenant, holding the left hand directly before his breast as is shown here above in the illustration noted 78 behind his hat.

The end of the guard and posture for the defending Provost.

In these following two illustrations the first strike is shown which is a maindroit *or thrust from above thrown by the Lieutenant against the Provost in order to make the first hold of this sword alone.*

[Images 79.80]

And in order to do it, this Lieutenant, having made the above-mentioned stance, guard and position is stood on the left foot and, stands there in order to execute this strike which is a *maindroit* or thrust from above. This next Lieutenant advanced the right foot and throws a *maindroit* or thrust, at his choice, against the Provost holding the fingers of the sword hand upwards and the left hand directly before his nose as is shown in the illustration numbered 79 behind the throat.

50. lit.: to be more near with it
51. ed: 80?

Thus, the end of the strike the that Lieutenant must throw at the Provost in order to make the first hold of this sword alone.

Here follows the teaching and defence from the first strike for the Provost in order to prepare himself to make the first hold which you see here after in the illustrations.

And in order to do this, having also made his stance and drawing (of the sword), the Provost should be stood in high guard being on the left foot, such as is drawn above in the illustration of the Provost numbered 78. And in order to defend himself from this *maindroit* or thrust from above that is thrown against him by the Lieutenant in order to show him the first hold which can be done and made against these strikes, this Provost, being on the left foot, has thrown the right foot behind and has crossed the Lieutenant's sword, strong on weak, lifting his sword point upwards a little and the left hand directly in front of the Lieutenant, holding the fingers of the sword hand upwards and the left hand before the breast, as is shown above in the illustration noted 80 behind the top of the head.

Thus the end of how the Provost defends against the above mentioned strike by the Lieutenant.

By these two following illustrations the attacking Lieutenant shows the defending Provost how he and all others should face the first hold of this sword alone and afterwards will show him the counter-holds and such.[52] *Anyone who will observe all that is said and that follows hereafter without omitting anything will never find himself surprised nor attacked and, if he find himself so, he ought to confess that it is not the fault of the author of the art but of having committed the fault himself, such that he who recognises his fault could be said to be learned even though he could not otherwise do it or teach it himself.*

I advise you, followers of Mars, that this art and science of arms has not been arranged in order to be abused but to conserve your honour and health. Because whoever will be ruled otherwise should not [?][53] the author nor the art. Thus to those who would abuse it and yet the wise dominate the others and those of bad will.[54]

---

52. *de sorte*
53. The verb appears to be missing
54. *mauvaise volontez*

The first strike, thrown on the maindroit or thrust from above, for the first hold by the Lieutenant and then executed by the Provost, as is shown here.

[Images 81.82]

And in order to do this, it is needed that this Lieutenant, having made his stance, guard and posture, being on the left foot, should advance the right foot as is shown in the figure and illustration above noted number 79. And also, this following Lieutenant, being on the left foot here above, advanced his right foot and threw a high thrust or *maindroit* to the Lieutenant,[55] holding the fingers of the sword hand upwards and this Lieutenant holds his left hand directly before his stomach below the sword arm as is shown in the illustration marked 81.

Thus the end of the strike which the Lieutenant threw in order to demonstrate to the Provost how to do the first hold of this sword alone.

Hereafter will be shown and explained how the Provost must and can make the first hold against the Lieutenant.

And in order to do this, the Provost, being on the left foot as the Lieutenant threw the *maindroit* or high thrust as he could, threw the left foot behind and crossed his sword with the Lieutenant's, strong on weak, turning the fingers of the sword hand upwards and in the same instant without any delay[56] advanced his left foot strongly forward and has gripped with his left hand the guard of the Lieutenant's sword and pretends to give him a turn in order to make him stop, as will be seen here after, holding the point of the sword directly at the forehead as is shown above in the illustration and figure noted with number 82.

Thus the end of the first hold next executed for the defending Provost against the Lieutenant.

The first hold, shown by the Lieutenant and in this strike also shown by him and executed by the Provost as is shown here.

[Images 83.84]

And in order for the Lieutenant to properly show how the Provost should do and execute this first hold, it is needed that the Lieutenant should be on the

55. ed: Provost?
56. *peu d'intervalle*

left foot, and, being there, advance the right foot and throw a *maindroit* or high thrust against the defending Provost. And being surprised by the Provost, who removed his sword from him, the Lieutenant was constrained to withdraw his right foot and to stand on the left foot and to hold his left hand before his breast, holding it ready to defend the point of the Provost's sword. The Lieutenant holds also his left hand against his left thigh, as is shown in the illustration noted with number 83 behind the throat.

Thus, all that the Lieutenant does in order to show to the Provost what he should do in order to execute all the first hold of this sword alone.

Here follows the first hold and its execution for the following Provost against the Lieutenant.

And in order to do this, the Provost, having made his first stance, guard and above-mentioned situation, that is to say, being on the left foot, and the Lieutenant having thrown at him a *maindroit* or high thrust as he may, should advance his right foot. And in order to make and execute this first hold for the following Provost, he has thrown his left foot backwards and has crossed the Lieutenant's sword, strong on weak, lifting a little the point of the sword upwards and at the same instant without any little interval, the Provost advances the left foot and with his left hand grabs the guard of the Lieutenant's sword, turning the top of it downwards, giving the turn in order to make him abandon the sword, and carrying it under the arm, presenting the sword point directly at the Lieutenant's mouth as is shown here above in the illustration noted 84.

Thus the end and demonstration from the Lieutenant and the execution of the first hold for the Provost.

In a hold he should make a counter-hold as is shown by the Lieutenant to the Provost.

[Images 85.86]

And in order to do this, the Lieutenant being on the left foot will throw a straight *maindroit* or thrust from above on the Provost's left side and in the same instant will turn to advance the left foot and will take the guard of the Provost's sword coming underneath his arm and, wanting to give the turn, the Provost made the counter hold which is exactly the same as was told and shown to him, as is here above in the illustration noted with number 85 behind his throat.

Thus the end for making the counter-hold for the Lieutenant.

Here follows the counter-hold for the Provost against the attacking Lieutenant.

And in order to do this, the Provost will be on the left foot in high guard and when the Lieutenant will advance the right foot in order to throw a *maindroit* or thrust from above, as he may at his choice, the Provost will throw the left foot backwards and will cross the *maindroit* or thrust thrown by the Lieutenant, strong on weak, and when he sees that the Lieutenant will advance the left foot in order to come to take the guard of the sword in order to make the first hold, the Provost, seeing this, in the same instant will advance the left foot and will take the guard of the Lieutenant's sword with his left hand, passing the sword under the arm, turning the top of the hand downwards and, having taken it, will pretend to turn this hand in order to remove the point of the sword as is shown here above in the illustration of the Provost, noted with number 86 behind the neck.

The end of the counter-hold for the Provost against the Lieutenant.

In the figures and illustrations which follow is shown how the counter-holds noted 85 and 86 are executed, both for the Lieutenant and the Provost, so that the Lieutenant, having carefully observed the will of the author, has removed entirely the Provost's sword and also the Provost having done the same, observing on his part that which he must do, to remove the Lieutenant's sword, so that one will see here after that the Lieutenant has the Provost's sword and the Provost has the Lieutenant's sword, as is noted in the illustrations with number 87 for the Lieutenant and 88 for the Provost.

Here follows the counter-hold, shown above by the Lieutenant and executed by the Provost.

[Images 87.88]

And in order to do this, the Lieutenant, being on the left foot as was said, will advance the right foot throwing a *maindroit* or thrust from above on the Provost and in the same time once again will advance the left foot and will take the Provost's sword underneath the right arm, turning the left hand, giving a turn in order to make him abandon the sword. And, seeing that the Provost was quick and clever even at the same time, this Lieutenant has withdrawn his left foot backwards and, holding the Provost's sword underneath his left arm, has immediately put his hand directly (or his right hand) to the point of the sword, pretending to put the sword on point as is shown in the illustration above noted with number 87 behind his head.

Thus the end of the counter-hold executed by the Lieutenant against the Provost.

Here follows a very good counter-hold for the Provost corresponding to the counter-hold made above by the Lieutenant.

And in order to do this, the following Provost will be on the left foot in high guard and, when the Lieutenant will advance the right foot as he can and must in order to throw a *maindroit* or thrust from above, the Provost will throw the left foot backwards and will cross the Lieutenant's sword, strong on weak, beating away the *maindroit* or high thrust that was thrown and, when he sees that the Lieutenant will advance the left foot in order to take the guard of the sword in order to make the hold, the Provost will advance the left foot at the same time as him and will take the guard of the Lieutenant's sword underneath his sword turning the left hand downwards as is shown in the illustration of the Provost noted with number 88.

Thus the end of the counter-hold for the Provost against the Lieutenant.

The posture and guard for the second hold for the Lieutenant against the Provost.

[Images 89.90]

And in order to do this, the Lieutenant having made one of the draws (unsheathings) is stood on the left foot in low guard, situating the point of his sword directly at the pants of the Provost, his pupil, making him do and stand[57] in medium guard. The Lieutenant holds the edge of the sword downwards and the left hand directly before his breast, as is shown above in the current illustration noted with number 89 behind the neck.

The end and definition of this low guard for the attacking Lieutenant.

After having treated above of the guard and posture of the Lieutenant, it remains to treat of the guard and posture of the defending Provost.

The Provost, after having made his stance, guard and situation, is stood on the

---

57. *tenir*

left foot in medium guard, holding the guard as high as the right shoulder and the fingertips of the sword hand downwards and he will hold the left hand on the left thigh – and all others which want to hold this guard will hold them and will make the gesture as this Provost – as is shown above in the illustration noted with number 90.

The end of the guard and posture for the Provost.

Hereafter the Lieutenant shows the Provost how he must do the second hold and yet the Lieutenant begins to do it.

The second hold for the demonstrating Lieutenant against the defending Provost.

[Images 91.92]

And in order to do this, the Lieutenant will do and will put himself as was said in low guard on the left foot situating the point of the sword as was said directly at the Provost's pants or belt, as was noted with numbers 89 and 90 in the illustrations above. And in order to do and execute this second hold for the Lieutenant, who is the attacking demonstrator, being in low guard as was said, will advance the right foot pretending to throw a *maindroit* or thrust from above. Coming from him, the Provost, seeing himself thus charged by such a strike, wants to defend himself, crossing and beating away the Lieutenant's sword. And thus the Lieutenant will advance the left foot and throw at him a backhand to the head. The Provost will want to beat it away immediately with his sword. Thus the Lieutenant will advance the left foot in the instant and will take the guard of the Provost's sword with his left hand and will threaten him with a thrust to the stomach, as is shown in the illustration noted with number 91 behind his neck.

Thus the end of the second hold and demonstration of it for the Lieutenant against the Provost.

Here follows that which the Provost must do for the second hold against the Lieutenant.

And in order to do this, the Provost is also on the left foot in middle guard as is noted above in illustration 90. The Lieutenant having thrown a *maindroit* or thrust from above, at his choice, the Provost threw the left foot backwards and crossed and beat away the Lieutenant's sword, strong on weak, and, seeing that he has been constrained by the Lieutenant's stance and hold, the following Provost, seeing this constraint, signalled with his left hand that he wants to turn and beat away the thrust that the Lieutenant wants and can do, as is shown above in the nearest illustration and drawing noted with number 92 at the back of the head.

The end of the second hold made by the Lieutenant on the Provost and that which he (the Provost) can do.

The second hold shown by the author to the Lieutenant and executed by him against the Provost to the end that he can do the same to another.

[Images 93.94]

And in order to do this, this following Lieutenant should, being on the right foot, advance the left foot and throw a *maindroit* or thrust from above on the Provost, stealing it[58] on the left-side, passing the sword underneath the guard of the Provost's sword and, in the same instant and tempo, he will advance the left foot and will cross the Provost's sword, strong on weak, and take the guard of the sword with his left hand, holding it, being drawn, and thus will be constrained to abandon it, seeing the point before him. And this all others will do when they will do the same, as is shown above in the illustration noted behind the throat with number 93.

Thus the end of the second hold shown and executed by the Lieutenant on the Provost.

And the Provost, seeing himself this surprised and pressed, observing the injury and danger which may occur, is constrained to leave the sword and throw his right foot backwards, preparing his right and left hands to beat away the thrust that the Lieutenant wants to throw at him. But he doesn't care[59] because the Lieutenant only does it in order to show him how he may do the above-mentioned holds on another, imitating well everything shown him by the Lieutenant, as is shown above in the illustration of the following Provost numbered 94 behind the throat.

Thus, that which the Provost must face and do for the second hold against the Lieutenant.

Hereafter will be shown by illustration and text how the Lieutenant has shown the

---

58. *le desobant*
59. *mais il n'a garde*

Provost, the Provost doing it to him as well, that there is nothing more which he knows to show.

The second hold as shown and executed by the Lieutenant and at present executed by the Provost against the Lieutenant as shown here.

[Images 95.96]

Here follows the demonstration of how this Lieutenant wants to show and make shown to perform on the Provost this second hold of the sword alone. And in order to do this, the following Lieutenant, being on the right foot, has thrown a straight *maindroit* or thrust from above to the Provost's left shoulder, advancing the left foot and, seeing the swiftness and surprise that by this means the Provost has executed the instruction, the Lieutenant has been constrained to withdraw his right foot and abandon the sword he had in his right hand and with his left hand beat away the Provost's sword. This Lieutenant guarded himself well if he wanted the Provost not to make this second on him hold but he pretends to be ignorant with the aim that the Provost makes this hold on him, as is shown above in the Lieutenant's illustration noted with number 95 behind his bonnet.

Thus the Lieutenant abandoned his sword seeing that the Provost has done as he was shown above well.

Here follows the demonstration of what the Provost must do in order to remove the sword from the Lieutenant following[60] *point by point the same which was shown and done in the above holds.*

And in order to do this, the Provost has made one of the four[61] draws (unsheathings), guard and positions and is standing on the left foot seeing that the Lieutenant threw at him a straight *maindroit* or thrust from above. The Provost, having well understood and remembered that which the Lieutenant did and showed to him, the Lieutenant having the same intention,[62] immediately and without pause crossed with his sword that of the Lieutenant, strong on weak, and threatened a thrust at his throat or nearby which has caused him to abandon

---

60. imitant
61. ed: three?
62. *coeur*

his sword, as is shown above in the Provost's illustration and drawing noted with number 96 behind the hat.

Thus the end of this second hold executed by the Provost against the Lieutenant, his instructor, having shown to him what[63] he must do.

Here follows the guard and posture in order to do the third hold for the Lieutenant against the Provost.

[Images 97.98]

And in order to do this, this Lieutenant having made of the four draws (unsheathings), as he may, is stood on the left foot in medium guard holding the fingers of the sword hand downwards, situating it directly at the Provost's left breast, holding the left hand on the left thigh as is shown above in the illustration noted with number 97 behind the hat.

Thus the end of the guard and posture for the Lieutenant in order to prepare himself to do this third hold against the Provost.

Hereafter is shown the guard and posture for the Provost.

The Provost's guard, in which he should have made the same draw as was said above one of the three draws (unsheathings), is and should be stood on the left foot for the first time. And seeing that the Lieutenant holds himself in middle guard, the Provost will hold himself in high guard situating the point of the sword directly at the Lieutenant's left eye, holding the sword hand with the fingers down and the sword flat such that a die can stand on it without falling from one side or the other[64] and so the sword's two quillions should be as high as each other and thus the sword should be in high guard, and medium,[65] otherwise one holds it falsely and breaks the rule[66] and it is not so good, being otherwise, the quillions of the sword will be falsely inverted, as is shown above in the illustration noted with number 98 behind the head.

Thus the end of the guard and posture for the Provost in order to throw the first strike for the third hold.

---

63. ed: *commē* = *comment*
64. *sans qu'il puisse ch(e)oir d'un coste ou autre*
65. *et moyenne*
66. lit: commits an incongruity

Here follows the first strike in order to do and show the third hold for the Lieutenant and Provost.

[Images 99.100]

And in order to do this, it is needed and necessary that the Lieutenant be on the left foot, having made all that which is required, that is to say, like the stance above and one of the three draws (unsheathings). And in order to execute this strike, he will advance the right foot and will throw a thrust from above to the Provost's left shoulder, holding the guard of the sword middlingly high, holding the fingers of the sword hand downwards and the left hand directly before the right breast as is shown above in the illustration noted with number 99. And in order to execute this third hold, in the same instant, the Lieutenant should, without advancing the left foot, take the guard of the defending Provost's sword, stretching out strongly with the left arm passing it above the right, holding the top of the hand upwards, giving the turn underneath the arm or elbow and threatening immediately a thrust to the Provost's face as is shown above in the illustration noted 99.

Thus the end of the third hold for the Lieutenant against the Provost.

Here follows the defence of this first strike in order to do and execute the third hold for the Provost against the Lieutenant.

And in order to do this, the Provost will have thus made one of the draws (unsheathings), guards and situations with the above stance and be standing on the left foot. And the Provost, seeing that the Lieutenant in the same instant has thrown at him a thrust from above, the Provost being on the left foot, threw it behind and has crossed the sword, with which the Lieutenant has thrown at him a *maindroit* or thrust from above, and defended it by this means: beating it away, strong on weak, holding the top of the sword hand downwards, situating the point directly at the Lieutenant's forehead, holding the left hand directly before and on the right thigh as is shown above in the illustration noted 100.

The end of the defence and teaching of this strike in order to prepare to do this third hold for the defending Provost.

The third hold shown and executed by this Lieutenant against the Provost with the end that the Provost will know how to do it to him and may do in the future and by consequence can do it to others.

[Images 101.102]

And in an instant without any small interval in order to gain time, having thrown the *maindroit* or thrust – as was said and shown above in the other illustrations noted with number 99 (not for this Lieutenant but for others) and 100 for the Provost. This Lieutenant should take the Provost's sword with his left hand, turning the top of this hand downwards and the palm upwards, holding the flat, fingers extended, pushing it along the arms to the elbow, lifting it high to make him abandon it and lose the point, as he did, threatening a thrust to the Provost's face, and in doing this he will be constrained to abandon the sword, as is shown above in the Lieutenant's illustration noted with number 101 behind the neck.

The end of the third hold for the Lieutenant against the Provost

Here follows that which the Provost must do, the Lieutenant showing him how to do it.

And in order to do this, the Lieutenant, having done as was said and discussed in several places above, which is as the Provost should have done, that is he has made one of the guards and draws (unsheathings) above and is stood on the left foot.[67] The Provost, seeing that the Lieutenant has advanced one step in order to throw at him a *maindroit* or thrust from above and all at once has taken the sword which the Provost was constrained to abandon it because the Lieutenant threatened a thrust at his face, holds his left hand directly before his left breast ready to beat away and turn aside the Lieutenant's sword, which is or should be a thrust to the face, as is all shown above in the following Provost's illustration noted with number 102 behind the bonnet.

Thus the end of the third hold made and executed by the Lieutenant and of that which the Provost could do, being thus surprised by the Lieutenant, his master.

---

67. This needs a lot of re-ordering to make sense. *Et pour ce faire, Iedit Lieutenant ayant fait comme dit est en plusieurs lieux, cy dessus et discouru, qui est que ledit Prevost doit avoir fait, comme il a une des gardes & deigainements cy dessus*

The third hold shown above by the Lieutenant to the Provost and is here executed by the Provost, as is evident.

[Images 103.104]

And in order to do this, having thrown at him a *maindroit* or thrust from above advancing the right foot, having done as is shown above in several strikes the stance, guard and position, such as pleases him,[68] immediately the Lieutenant having thrown the *maindroit* or high thrust, the Provost has with such diligence executed this hold causing the Lieutenant to be constrained to abandon his sword. And seeing that the Provost wants to throw a thrust to his belly, the Lieutenant, as was said, was forced to abandon his sword, the left hand feigning to beat away the Provost's sword as is shown above in the illustration noted with number 103.

Thus the end of the counter-hold which the Provost has done to the Lieutenant, as it appears.

Here-after follows what the Provost must do in order to execute the third hold against the Lieutenant.

And in order to do this, the Provost being in the stance of the left foot, the Lieutenant will throw a *maindroit* or thrust from above, as he chooses,[69] on the Provost's left shoulder or left breast. But in order to counter[70] whatever strikes he could throw, the Provost should and needs to throw his left foot backwards and cross with his sword the Lieutenant's sword, strong on weak, and on the same right foot in the same instant, the Provost will pass the sword below the Lieutenant's sword and will let the point fall over the Lieutenant's arm and immediately will take in his left hand the Lieutenant's sword. He will lift upwards the flat of his hand having passed it below the elbow in order to make him lose it from his hand, threatening him with a thrust to his belly as is shown in the Provost's illustration noted with number 105 behind the neck.

Thus the end of the third hold for the following defending Provost against the Lieutenant.

Hereafter will be shown the stance and guard for the Lieutenant and Provost in order

68. *telle que luy à pleu*
69. *à sa liberté*
70. *anuller*

to make and execute the fourth and last hold of this sword alone. There are others and in the other edition nothing will be left out.

The stance and guard for the fourth and last hold for the attacking Lieutenant against the defending Provost.

[Images 105.106]

And to deal well with this above-mentioned guard and fourth hold for the Lieutenant, he should have thus made the stance, one of the draws (unsheathings) and the guard above. And in this example here,[71] it is required that the Lieutenant be on the left foot in high guard holding the top of the sword hand upwards and the fingers downwards, situating the sword point directly at the Provost mouth, holding the left hand on his left hip as is shown above in the illustration noted with number 105.

The end of the guard in order to make a strike for executing this fourth hold for the Lieutenant.

It will be shown hereafter the guard and stance in order to defend a strike which will be a maindroit *or thrust from above thrown by the Lieutenant against the Provost in order to do the fourth hold.*

In order to do this, having made one of the three draws (unsheathings) and being on the left foot, the Provost will hold himself in medium guard, which is the best,[72] holding the top of the sword hand upwards, situating the point of it directly at the Lieutenant's left breast, and the left hand directly before his hip, as is shown above in his illustration noted with number 106.

Thus the end of the description and stance for the Provost.

The maindroit *or thrust from above thrown by the Lieutenant and defended by the Provost, which should be repeated*[73] *by the Lieutenant in order to execute the fourth hold against the Provost.*

[Images 107.108]

71. *cestuy cy*
72. *la plus superlative*
73. lit.:thrown again

And in order to do this, this following Lieutenant should be on the left foot in high guard as is shown above in his other illustration noted with number 105, seen in its place. And in order to execute this strike, which is a *maindroit* or thrust from above at the Lieutenant's choice, he will advance the right foot and will throw a straight thrust to the Provost's face, holding the guard of the sword as high as the right shoulder and the top of the sword hand downwards and the left hand in front of his chin, as is shown above in the illustration noted with number 107.

The end of this strike for the attacking Lieutenant.

The means of defending oneself by the Provost from this maindroit or thrust from above thrown by the Lieutenant in order to then after execute the fourth hold.

And in order to do this, the following Provost should be on the left foot in middle guard as is shown above in the his illustration noted with number 106. And for the defence of this *maindroit* or thrust from above thrown by the Lieutenant, the Provost should and is required to throw the left foot backwards and cross his sword with that of the Lieutenant, be it a *maindroit* or thrust from above, strong on weak as was done above in one of the oppositions and follow-ups, and threaten a thrust to the Lieutenant's face, holding the top of the sword hand downwards and the fingers upwards and the left hand directly before his breast, situating the sword point directly at the Lieutenant's mouth, as is shown and done above in the Provost's illustration noted behind the throat with number 108.

Thus how the Provost guards himself well from the above strike thrown by the Lieutenant.

Hereafter will be shown the fourth and last hold, which is very subtle in order to make his adversary abandon his weapons, which will be by means of a maindroit *or high thrust which one will throw, which will serve to discover ignorance or knowledge.*[74] *Because, if he is ignorant and unskilled, he should do it simply, and if he is skilful, he should make a feint as will be seen hereafter in its place in the Lieutenant's explanation which will be for showing it to the Provost.*

The fourth hold shown by the attacking Lieutenant to the defending Provost as clearly shown here and explained below in writing.

74. *qu'il servira d'espion pour apporter ignorance ou scavoir*

[Images 109.110]

And in order to do this, the Lieutenant, being on the left foot as is shown above in the illustration in the stance and guard noted above with number 105, advanced the right foot and threw a probing[75] *maindroit* or thrust from above on the Provost's left side, as was said and shown above in the Lieutenant's illustration noted with number 107. And this Lieutenant, seeing that the Provost has defended himself from this *maindroit* or thrust from above, in order to do this hold the following Lieutenant has from a *maindroit* stolen his sword underneath the Provost's sword and this Lieutenant has let his sword fall above the Provost's arm, turning the fingers of the sword hand upwards and with the left hand holding the Provost's sword near the point. This done, the Lieutenant speaks to the Provost and tells him "listen, if I want to lower and weigh down my left hand, you will be constrained to abandon your sword as you can and in fact will do to me", as is shown above in the Lieutenant's next illustration and drawing noted with number 109.

Thus the end of the fourth and last hold for the demonstrating Lieutenant against the defending Provost.

Here follows that which the Provost could do, not knowing any counter-hold, because to every hold there is a counter-hold, not that which was done above but that which will be done below through the information[76] that the Lieutenant gave him.

And in order to do this, the following Provost is on the left foot in middle guard as is shown above in the illustration noted with number 106. The Provost, in order to learn to do this above-mentioned hold, threw the left foot behind and is stood on the right foot and has crossed the *maindroit* or thrust from above that was thrown by the Lieutenant. But the Lieutenant, having avoided it by a stolen *maindroit* in order to complete his hold, has made[77] the Provost at the conclusion[78] abandon his sword and, if he wanted to, has made him lose his hand. But allowing it to him again, however, the Provost has done as he could, being deceived as is shown above in the illustration noted with number 110.

The end of that which the Provost could do against the Lieutenant, his instructor.

---

75. *pour espion*
76. *intelligence*
77. *a rendu*
78. *extremite*

The fourth and last hold executed by the defending Provost against the Lieutenant, his instructor, as shown here plainly by the illustration, showing him that which was done above.

[Images 111.112]

And in order to do it, this Lieutenant should be on the left foot, as was said above, and advancing the right foot will throw a *maindroit* or thrust from above, at his choice, as is shown above in the other illustration of the same Lieutenant noted with number 107. This Lieutenant has thrown one of the strikes. This Provost did the same as that above. The Lieutenant did to him as evident in the illustration noted with number 109 but, in this hold here, the Lieutenant has been constrained to abandon his sword and with his left hand wants to beat away the Provost's sword, who wants to throw a thrust at him as evident in the illustration above noted with number 111 behind the throat.

The end of that which this Lieutenant has done, having shown the Provost what he needs to face this hold.

Here follows the execution of this fourth and last hold of this sword alone for the Provost against the Lieutenant, his instructor.

And in order to do this, the following Provost is on the left foot and when he sees that the Lieutenant or other attacker should throw a *maindroit* or thrust from above, advancing the right foot, the Provost will throw his left foot backwards and in the same instant will steal his sword underneath the guard of the Lieutenant's sword and, with very little interval, will let fall the point of the sword on that of the Lieutenant. Immediately the Provost will take the point of the Lieutenant's sword with his left hand and will pass and lower it down and thus will constrain the Lieutenant to abandon his sword, as is shown above in the Provost's illustration noted with number 112.

Thus the end of this fourth and last hold of the sword alone both for the attacking Lieutenant as for the defending Provost.

Hereafter will be shown some good and subtle individual strikes extracted from the above strikes of the sword alone which I call the subtleties which can be done and made both in attacking and in defending.

The guard and stance in order to do and execute the subtleties of this sword alone, as much for the attacking Lieutenant as for the defending Provost.

[Images 113.114]

And in order to do this, it is necessary that the demonstrating Lieutenant, having made one of the draws (unsheathings), stances, guards and situations, will be on the left foot in high guard[79] holding the sword hand as high as the right shoulder, the top of it upwards and the fingers downwards, situating the point of the sword at the Provost's face and the left hand below his sword arm, as is shown above in the illustration noted with number 113 behind the bonnet.

The end of the stance and guard for the attacking Lieutenant.

Here follows the definition, guard and stance for the Provost.

And in order to do this, the Provost should make one of the draws (unsheathings), such as pleases him, and hold himself on the left foot in low guard holding the guard of the sword on his left knee, situating the point of it directly at the Lieutenant's belt or pants, the edge downwards and the left hand directly before the left breast as is shown above in the illustration noted with number 114.

The end of the guard for the Provost.

The first cut, which is a low maindroit, thrown by the Lieutenant against the Provost, which serves to discover in order to expose ignorance or knowledge.

[Images 115.116]

And in order to do this, the Lieutenant is on the left foot in high guard, as is shown above in his said guard and posture of the subtleties noted with number 113. And in order to do and properly execute this subtlety for the demonstrating Lieutenant, he will advance the right foot and will throw a low *maindroit* to the knee, which serves discovery in order to expose the ignorance or knowledge of him against whom such a strike will be thrown, because, if he is ignorant, he will cross sword against sword and, if he is knowledgeable, he will throw a *maindroit* on the sword arm. But it is good to see that this Provost is ignorant as he crosses his sword with that of the Lieutenant, showing to the Provost the fault which he has made, beating away the sword instead of throwing a *main-*

---

79. ed: this is actually the definition of medium guard, not high guard

droit on the arm, as he will do hereafter. But in this strike he crosses the sword, as is shown above in his illustration noted with number 115.

Thus the Lieutenant threw a low maindroit to the knee in order to see ignorance.

Here follows the defence of this strike for the Provost.

And in order to do it, the Provost should have done the same step, guard and position that is shown above in the Provost's illustration noted with number 114. And in order to defend himself from this strike, which is a low *maindroit* to the knee thrown at him by the Lieutenant, the Provost, being ignorant – as are many demonstrators – has thrown the left foot behind and has crossed the Lieutenant's sword with his sword, which is to presume ignorance but not entirely, understanding that he has set aside the proper and taken the improper, which is said and shown above in the illustration noted with number 116 behind the Provost.

Thus how the Provost defends himself against the first strike thrown by the Lieutenant. But he defends himself from it, as intended and as shown often following human nature, because it does the same without ever knowing the art.

The guard and posture for the Lieutenant and Provost in order for the Lieutenant to show the Provost how he should do it instead and not as he did in the previous strike.

[Images 117.118]

And in order to do this, it is necessary that this Lieutenant, having made one of the three draws (unsheathings) whichever pleases him, is stood on the left foot in medium guard, situating the point of his sword directly at the left breast, holding the top of the sword hand upwards and the left hand below the sword arm, as is shown above in the illustration noted with number 117.

The end of the Lieutenant's guard in order to do and execute this subtlety following the ignorance which the Lieutenant has shown the Provost noted with number 115 and 116.

Here follows the text for knowing to do the Provost's stance and guard in order to execute this subtlety, by the Lieutenant, showing it to the Provost, as will be seen hereafter in the next strike.

And in order to do this, the following Provost should have made the stance that was made by the following Lieutenant above, his demonstrator, and one of the draws (unsheathings) and be standing on the left foot in high guard, holding also the guard of the sword and the sword hand upwards, situating the point directly at the face, holding the left hand directly before his breast, as is shown above in the Provost's illustration notes with number 118.

Thus the end of the guard and posture for the Provost.

The first strike of this subtlety, which is on the first strike of the sword alone, here shown by this Lieutenant and executed by this Provost.

[Images 119.120]

This current Lieutenant, in order to do well and show to the Provost this *maindroit*, the first strike of the program of the sword alone and of this subtlety, being on the left foot, should advance the right foot and throw a low *maindroit* to the Provost's knee, holding his left hand directly before the face, as is shown here above in the illustration noted with number 119.

The end of this first strike which is a maindroit from below thrown by this following Lieutenant and defended by the Provost and executed by him, there where he should.

Here follows all that the Provost should do in order to defend himself and offend at the same time this low maindroit to the knee thrown by the Lieutenant against the Provost.

And in order to do this, the Provost is in high guard, as is shown above in the other illustration numbered 118. And now this Provost, having seen that the Lieutenant has thrown a low *maindroit* at him to the left knee, this time[80] recognises that he did poorly to beat away the sword and that the only stance sufficient to protect against this *maindroit*. And at this time this Provost threw the left foot behind in the same instant defended this *maindroit* coming from high guard on the Lieutenant's sword arm and presented then[81] a thrust at the Lieutenant's belly, holding the guard of the sword somewhat high and the fingers of this hand upwards and his left hand directly before his left breast, as is shown above in the illustration numbered 120.

80. *à ce coup*
81. *encores*

The end of this subtlety for the Provost and of all that which he should do following the instruction of the author and of his Lieutenant.

The guard and low posture in order to execute and do the second strike of these subtleties, which is a renvers from below, being on the right foot which serves to discover in order to expose ignorance or knowledge, both for the attacking Lieutenant as for the defending Provost.

[Images 121.122]

For executing well and dexterously this second subtlety for the Lieutenant, he should have made one of the draws (unsheathings) and in order to throw this second strike the Lieutenant should be on the right foot in low guard, the edge of the sword downwards and the guard of the sword on his left hip, situating the sword point directly at the Provost's right thigh, holding the left hand directly before his pants,[82] as is shown above in the illustration numbered 121.

The end of the declaration of the guard for the Lieutenant.

Here follows the guard and posture for the Provost and the declaration of such.

And in order to do this, the Provost should have made the same drawing (of the sword) and similar[83] guard and hold himself and be on the right foot, holding the sword guard on his right thigh, situating the sword point directly at the Lieutenant's pants or nearby, holding the edge of the sword downwards and holding his left hand near his belt, the fingertips near his pants, as is shown above in the illustration numbered 122.

The end of the posture for the Provost.

The second strike, which is a renvers from below, *serves to discover*[84] *for doing and executing better the second subtlety for the Lieutenant against the Provost.*

[Images 123.124]

And in order to do this, the Lieutenant should be on the right foot in low guard,

---

82. *la brayette*
83. *presque*
84. *pour espion*

as is noted above in other illustrations and noted for this Lieutenant with number 121. And being in this stance and guard, he pretends[85] to throw a thrust to the Provost's face and in the same instant advances his left foot and throws a backhand to the Provost's right knee, holding the guard of the sword a little high and holding the left hand below the sword arm, as is shown above in the illustration noted with number 123 behind the bonnet.

The end of the strike, which is a renvers from below, which serves to discover for the Lieutenant to expose ignorance, as it does, and not knowledge.

Here follows that which the Provost does in order to defend this renvers from below thrown by the Lieutenant.

And in order to do this, the Provost is also on the right foot in low guard, as is shown in the illustration numbered 122 and this Lieutenant advances the left foot in order to throw a backhand from below to the Provost's knee. Seeing himself attacked[86] like this, the Provost throws his right foot backwards and crossed with his sword that of the Lieutenant, as the ignorant and even today all ignorant demonstrators do but the skilful and learned no longer do – at least they should no longer do – because they win the tempo in all things and principally in this art of arms, as will be shown hereafter. This Provost holds his left hand directly before his breast, as is shown in the illustration numbered 124.

The end of the false strike which the following Provost does because it was left suitable and takes the unsuitable.

The second strike which is a renvers on the Provost's arm thrown and executed by this current Lieutenant against the Provost, showing him what he could do and not to beat away the sword, as he has done above, in the following[87] illustrations.

[Images 125.126]

And in order to do this, this Lieutenant is on the right foot in low guard, as was said and shown above noted with number 121. And the Lieutenant being on the right foot will pretend to throw a thrust to the Provost's face and will advance the left foot pretending to throw a backhand to the knee. The Provost wants to

---

85. *face semblant*
86. *chargé*
87. read: previous?

beat it away as he did sword against sword. This Lieutenant, seeing this, lifts his sword and throws a backhand to the elbow of his sword arm, holding his left hand below his sword arm as is shown above in the illustration numbered 125 behind his bonnet.

The end of this renvers executed and demonstrated by the Lieutenant to the Provost.

Here follows that which the Provost does.

The Provost is on the right foot in low guard as is noted in the illustration numbered 122. The Provost must, in throwing his right foot backwards, throw a *renvers* on the Lieutenant's arm and not cross the Lieutenant's sword with his sword, as he did returning to beat it away as in the above strike – which caused the Lieutenant to throw a *renvers* on the elbow of his sword arm. And this Provost holds his left hand directly before his left breast as is shown above in the illustration numbered 126 behind his neck.

The end of that which the Provost does against the Lieutenant in order to defend this second subtlety.

Here follows another very good and subtle strike, neglecting the renvers *on the arm and coming from a thrust to the belly, crossing strong on weak the Provost's sword, as is shown here by the author to the Provost and, by consequence, the Provost will learn from the Lieutenant.*

Another very good and subtle strike for the Lieutenant against the Provost, neglecting the backhand on the elbow and throwing a thrust to the belly as is shown here.

[Images 127.128]

In order to properly do and execute this thrust,[88] which is a subtle and very good strike, it is required that this Lieutenant should be on the right foot and, being there, advance his left foot and pretend[89] to throw a low backhand at the Provost's knee. The Provost will think to beat it away. Thus the Lieutenant will advance his left foot and instead throw it on the arm, as he did in the preceding strike, crossing strongly in the middle of his sword that of the Provost and threatening him with a thrust to the stomach, holding his left hand below

---

88. *ce coup en estoc*
89. *fera semblant*

the elbow of his sword arm as is shown above in the illustration numbered 127 behind the feather in his hat.

Thus that which the Lieutenant must do in order to execute and demonstrate this strike in the form of a thrust at the Provost.

Here follows that which the Provost must do for the last strike of this sword alone.

And this next and last Provost in this entire treatise being on the right foot, seeing that the Lieutenant wants to throw at him a low backhand to the knee, the Provost threw the right foot behind and thinking to throw a backhand on the Lieutenant's sword arm, as has been shown by him above in the illustration of the Provost which is numbered 125. Here the Provost finds himself frustrated in the execution of his *renvers*, which he thought well done whereas the Lieutenant beat it away, strong on weak, and threatened him with a thrust. But this has been done by the Lieutenant showing the Provost that he can do both above-mentioned strikes, *renvers* thrusts, and this last Provost holds his left hand directly before his breast in order to beat away the Lieutenant's sword, given that he crossed him strong on weak, and he can not defend it nor throw a thrust except with his left hand, as is shown above in the illustration numbered 128 near the feather in his bonnet.

Thus the end of the defence of this strike for the last Provost against the Lieutenant and all the others contained in this treatise on this sword alone, as was said, the mother of all arms.

Made and composed by Henry de Sainct-Didier, esquire, Provencal gentleman.

Hereafter follows a treatise composed by the author which compares[90] tennis with swordsmanship with the points and reasons here below explained.

---

90. lit: is about

[Jeu de Paulme and Swordsmanship]

Here follows a treatise on the practice of and certain points required to know about the game of tennis for all those who love it, composed by the author, considering that it requires the same stance and understanding, the same strikes as swordsmanship,[1] as will be shown here in this treatise, written[2] by the author because of the affinity and sympathy they have together, both for counselling and instructing[3] the unlearned and those who do not understand the terms of this exercise and not for the learned and skilful.

The author considers that tennis and swordsmanship are very close first cousins, as was said above, and whoever well knows how to play tennis easily can learn to throw sword strikes and their oppositions. But one, which is swordsmanship, merits more than the other because it preserves the health and honour of those who fear to lose them. Someone could ask why swordsmanship and tennis are first cousins. The author responds to this and says that the same strikes that one throws in swordplay in order to vanquish his enemy in times of peace or of war are the same strikes one can use to vanquish his competitor[4] when he wants to compete[5] for winning himself money or glory,[6] which are:

- *Maindroit*
- *Renvers*
- Thrust

Well is it true that one of these strikes should be removed, which is the thrust, and only two will remains, which are:

- *Maindroit*
- *Renvers*

The reason why I remove the thrust is, considering the racket has no point, thus one cannot know how to thrust.

It is true that sometimes one makes a strike and beat-away[7] with the racket

---

1. *armes*
2. lit: made
3. *bailler advertissement & instruction*
4. *sa partie adverse*
5. lit: make some match
6. *quelque banquet* - lit: a seat at the table

when the ball[8] comes straight at the face or above, which is that one turns away the ball, and the beat-away with the racket when it comes from above or to the face, holding it directly in front, not deviating to either the right side or the left side. Although in this game of tennis there are only two shots, the *maindroit* and *renvers,* they enumerate themselves into four items, high and low, such as *maindroit* low and *maindroit* high, *renvers* low and *renvers* high. Thus one must know how to throw them very dexterously and gracefully since they perform here as well as they do as in swordsmanship. And knowing how to dexterously throw [weapons] one should observe what our ancestors said "tennis players (they say) that because of the rebound abandon the volley, will never be considered good players", that is to say everyone should take here good counsel, which is that when one takes the volley, one should never wait for the bounce. The reason for this is that the rebound may happen in several ways but never in the volley, ever, if one is practised, and that is sure.

The occurrence which can happen in the volley is to beat it[9] away with the wood of the racket. This is not an accident but a fault committed by him who hits with the wood and not the inside of the racket on the ball. In this case, I want to counsel those who are not yet sure of the rebound, who practice the volley yet shouldn't, and those who fail at it. And if necessary, one has again recourse to the rebound and although those who can should always take the volley and not the rebound.

Hereafter will be explained the points which are fundamental to this game and the practice of tennis which should be well observed.

The first requirement for one who wants to attack another and to compete for high stakes,[10] is taking shoes with lead soles or heavy weights and carrying them for two or three hours before commencing his match. This time passed, he comes to leave the heavy soles and content himself with his shoes. When he conducts himself in light shoes it may be well to his advantage[11] and, in doing this, as such, will find himself better disposed and more dexterous than those that did not do it, practice being the master of all arts.

The second requirement in this game is to ask first for the rackets and to choose

 7. *rabat*
 8. *eteuf*
 9. ie: the ball
 10. *faire partie de consequence*
 11. *à son point*

the best and that is light and comfortable in the hand. And it is the same in swordsmanship which requires a light sword and heavy dagger, as in tennis one should have a light racket and heavy ball, neither too heavy nor too light because all things which are too heavy or too light are worth nothing.

The third point that is required and should be well regarded is that whenever one is in a game of tennis having another racket with which we want to help and say to the opposing party, "let's toss the racket in order to see who will be inside or outside"[12] and then they will say "toss yours". If he give you the liberty, throw the worst and not the good one as will be hereafter explained. If he would throw his, let him throw it because in throwing it the sinews[13] weaken themselves. In weakening itself, it damages itself inasmuch as the sinews stretch themselves and thus it cannot be used as well as it was before. One could say, "we will demand another of them." In response, in this possibility, one could not find it so well in the hand as that one which had been found before.[14] One wants to guard against this because very often a racket is the advantage[15] in the match as a good sword is also the advantage by which one conquers his enemy.

Fourth item, having well observed all that was said, it remains to know on which stance he should hold himself in order to well execute the art of tennis in order to serve the ball well on the tiles[16] and to give as difficult a game as we can throughout the match.[17] I say that in order to practice well all these strikes being enumerated and in order to serve well, he should hold himself on the left foot for the first time and always make any repositioning[18] on it, looking for the ball on whichever side it will go. Anyone can say I do not know where the ball will go and cannot determine it. It should be considered that when anyone judges where the ball will be thrown by their opponent,[19] keeping it in view and by this judging where he wants to throw it, it is very good. But I will give one which will be better and the obvious reason. This judgement is often deceptive because by sight, one cannot judge surely that which the will[20] wants to do and execute, which is directing and throwing the ball. I say that in order to

12. positions on the tennis court?
13. *les cordes*
14. ie: the previous racket or one's own racket
15. *le gain*
16. A reference to Royal Tennis in which bouncing the ball off the walls was permitted?
17. *donner mauvais jeu le plus qu'on pourra tout le long du jeu*
18. *la pirouette*
19. *leur partie adverse*
20. lit: interior

effectively[21] judge the ball, where the opponent could throw it, he should not look at the face because the opponent will deceive you with it. But look well at the ball which has been served and never lose it from sight. Because the ball, which is external to the will[22] is directed and managed without falsehood[23] by the interior and will of your opponent and, being sure of your hand, without fault you will conquer your opponent easily. Do not look at the face because, looking at it, you will think that he throws the ball to you on the opposite side to his glance and his interior will be otherwise and thus looking at the face of your opponent you could be deceived and looking at the ball you never will be. And this is the argument that I said in arms by which you should look at the point of the sword and not the face of the man.

I have not put forth these reasons for those who understand them but to the contrary for those who do not understand them.

I have really wanted to talk of tennis because one worthy, who is one of the good players of it, has been to see me only two or three times and having learned two or three strikes, he increased his score[24] to nearly fifteen. This worthy throws forehands and backhands with very good grace. Thus tennis and swordsmanship, as said, have a great affinity.

Dear Reader

Whomever among you would buy these books and find not the name, surname and titles of the author written there in his hand, such books were not sold by his intention. In this cause, he prays you bring them to him at his house and he will return the money that they cost you, naming him who sold them to you and, if you will give so much, take the author to the seller, which will cost you nothing. Finally, the author will show you and explain the contents of the books which will cost you nothing in order to have recourse to justice for the opposition of those who would sell such books and to please him.

H. de Sainct-Didier

---

21. *bien*, lit: well
22. lit: *l'exterior*
23. *sans fallace*
24. *adresse*

Dear Reader

The author knows that swordsmanship and the law are two very necessary virtues with which to acquire[1] the friendship of kings, princes, lords and even ladies. In this cause, the author has preferred to choose of them the art and practice of arms rather than the law. Not that he has abandoned everything, but exercising in them for 30 years and after long days, God given him the grace, he has dedicated and actually presented this treatise to one of the grandest Christian monarchs who may be under heaven. And by his commandment has fought with his highness in arms and with Monseigneur Duke de Guise and others of his court, of which the author has praised and praises god, who has made this boon that he has had the luck and favour which Sire has given him of printing it and putting it into the light for the solace and contentment of his nobility and public good. There may be many others who would slander and warn against the author, by reason of his treatise and other little speeches that he has made on the exercise and game of tennis. The author has not treated of that which was said for those who are skilled and tested and who understand the true terms which are required in both practices – that is to say, swordsmanship and tennis – but for those who do not understand.

In this cause, the author asks the readers to want only to take it in good faith and excuse it and neither looking at the language nor at the letter and surface[2] of it, and in the time it will be resolved. Yet such as will speak against it or want to slander it who have been taught or have known to do as much, and having seen and heard speak the author, who could discuss with them[3] the reasons and show by examples the contents of the treatise, the naysayers[4] (if any be found) can themselves find the contents, advice and judgements[5] demonstrate in the words and in the actions. They do not yet they address themselves to the author who could make them content by reason of his report.

This treatise was printed[6] on 4 June 1573.

1. *à faire acquerir*
2. *escorce*
3. lit: you
4. *contredisans*
5. *arestez -*
6. *a esté achevé d'imprimer*

Table of this Tract on the Sword Alone

Tract containing the secrets of the first books on the sword alone, mother of all weapons
Portrait of the King   fo.1 folio 1
Epistle to the King   fo.2
It follows the secrets of this sword alone and all other weapons which depend on it in order to understand them and above all better execute the six required points   fo.3
First   fo.3
Second   fo.3
Third   fo.3
Fourth   fo.3
Fifth   fo.3
By the Sixth   fo.3
It follows hereafter the explanations and reasons for the six points   fo.4
The reason for the first   fo.4
The second is knowing how many guards   fo.4
The third point is…   fo.4
Well is it true that they can be enumerated in six items   fo.4
The fourth point   fo.5
It follows the named of the six targets where one should and can throw the three strikes, that is to say the maindroit, renvers and thrust   fo.5
The first strike and target   fo.5
The second strike and target   fo.5
The third target   fo.5
The fourth target   fo.5
The fifth target   fo.5
The sixth is, that he should know to defend himself and attack at the same time of the three strikes: to deliver and throw to the places, both for the defender as for the attacker, observing well the time required   fo.5
The sixth and last point is one of the best   fo.5
The reason for judging one of the strikes   fo.5
Thus the end and explanation of the sixth and last point   fo.5
Following the six points, one named Fabrice and Jules came to me one time   fo.5
And then I attacked Fabrice   fo.6
And thus responded Fabrice   fo.6
Sainct-Didier responds and says that all response …   fo.6
And this Fabrice, seeing …   fo.6
And seeing this response offered by Fabrice   fo.6
Thus the author   fo.6
Response of the author   fo.6
If one said or questioned a master of the camp and one asked how many avenues the enemy
And in order to respond and conclude to this that above was said   fo.6 fo.6
It follows the explanation and reasons hereafter why the author removes the fendente   fo.7

Hereafter is also the reason why the author removes the imbroccata from the five strikes	fo.7
The reason	fo.7
Thus, the end of all that which is required and necessary to know and understand by each who wants to be skilful at arms	fo.7
For giving understanding of weapons and to discourse on the art, program and practice of them	fo.7
By the author will be described hereafter all the program what he must hold the Lieutenant and Provost	fo.8
To the King by Estienne de la Guette, gentleman of arms and of arts	fo.8
Egyptians and Greeks	fo.9
The handling of the sword	fo.10
A meeting with thugs	fo.10
Your France in good skill	fo.11
Sonnet to the author by M. de l'aigle	fo.11
Sonnet by Jacques Brocher, mathematician of Pertuz in Provence to the author	fo.12
By Jean Emery, Provencal from Berre, to Henry de Sainct-Didier, Provencal gentleman, a sonnet	fo.12
Elegy composed by Pierre du Fief, Poitevin, lawyer	fo.13
Making his son, the second Mars, a gift	fo.13
However, I support [supplie] you to advance your step	fo.14
The one will think in the heart, the other will say out loud	fo.14
Sonnet by Pierre Quinefort, Poitevin	fo.15
Sonnet	fo.15
Sonnet by Estienne duFour to M. Sainct-Didier	fo.16
Sonnet to the Supporters of Mars	fo.16
Sonnet to M. Sainct-Didier, Provencal gentleman, by M. de Vaulusien	fo.17
Sonnet to the author	fo.17
Sonnet	fo.18
Sonnet	fo.18
The figure and portrait of the King	fo.19
Sonnet to the King	fo.19
Portrait of the author	fo.20
Sonnet to the author by Amadis Iamim, King's Secretary	fo.20
It follows hereafter how he should stand in order to properly draw the sword,[1] both in times of peace as in times of war	fo.21
Hereafter in four footprints are put and situated below the feet of the Lieutenant and Provost Stance and general outline	fo.21 fo.21
Explanation of the outline and stance for the Provost	fo.22
Guard for making and executing the first stance, first and second drawing (of the sword), for the Lieutenant and Provost	fo.22
It follows the second drawing (of the sword) for the Lieutenant	fo.23
Hereafter is explained the first and second drawing (of the sword) for the Provost, who wants to know how to properly draw the sword[2] as shown him by the Lieutenant	fo.23

---

1. *mettre l'espee au poing*
2. *qui est pour scavior bien mettre les armes au poing*

It follows for the Provost[3] the second drawing (of the sword)	fo.23
After having shown the above…	fo.24
Guard and stance in order to start to do the third drawing (of the sword) for the Lieutenant demonstrating to the defending Provost	fo.24
The third drawing (of the sword) for the Lieutenant	fo.24
The end of the beginning of the third drawing (of the sword) for the Lieutenant	fo.25
The end of the third drawing (of the sword) for the Lieutenant and Provost	fo.25
In order to well and with grace achieve the third drawing (of the sword)	fo.25
The end of the achievement of the third drawing (of the sword) for the Lieutenant	fo.26
And for the achievement of the third drawing (of the sword)	fo.26
General stance, both the the attacking Lieutenant as for the the defending Provost in order to execute the art, program and practice contained in this sword alone	fo.26
In order to show and explain his general stance for the Lieutenant	fo.26
It follows the outline and stance that the defending Provost should make being instructed by the Lieutenant	fo.27
And in order to do this, the Provost should be similarly placed with feet together	fo.27
Stance and guard of this first strike of the sword alone for the Lieutenant	fo.27
Text for the first guard and stance for the Provost in order to start the program of this sword alone	fo.28
This guard is nearly the same as the above	fo.28
To explain [pour declarer] this guard for the Lieutenant	fo.28
It follows that which the Provost must do	fo.29
It follows the first strike of the sword alone for the attacking Lieutenant against the defending Provost	fo.29
Hereafter is explained how the Provost has defended his knee	fo.30
It follows the first opposition and follow-up of the first strike	fo.30
Hereafter will be explained the defence of the first opposition and follow-up for the Provost against the Lieutenant	fo.31
It follows the second opposition and follows-up for the attacking Lieutenant against the defending Provost	fo.31
Hereafter will be shown how the Provost must defend the second opposition and follow-up	
In these two illustrations which follow will be shown the guard and stance in order to do the second strike for the Lieutenant and Provost, following the program of this sword alone	fo.32
It follows the text of the guard and stance for the Provost	fo.33 fo.32
It follows the second strike of this sword alone	fo.33
Hereafter is explained the second strike of this sword alone for the Provost	fo.34
It follows the oppositions and follow-ups and explanations of them for the second strike, which is a low renvers to the Provost's left knee thrown by the Lieutenant	fo.34
Hereafter will be shown the explanation of the first opposition or follow-up of the second strike	fo.35
Explanation of the second opposition of the second strike for the Lieutenant and Provost	
And if any Lieutenants or Provosts should be left-handers	fo.36 fo.36
It follows the guard and stance for the third strike which is a high maindroit for the attacking Lieutenant against the defending Provost	fo.36

3. *par iceluy Provost*

It follows the guard and stance for the third strike for the defending Provost fo.37
The third strike of this sword alone for the Lieutenant and Provost is a high maindroit, following the above-mentioned program items[4] fo.37
Hereafter is the explanation and defence of the third strike, which is a high maindroit, thrown by the attacking (Lieutenant) and defended by the Provost fo.38
It follows the first opposition and follow-up for the Lieutenant and Provost for the third strike of this sword alone fo.38
It follows the defence of the first opposition and follow-up of the third strike for the Provost against the Lieutenant fo.39
Second opposition and follow-up of the third strike for the Lieutenant and Provost fo.39
Hereafter is shown and explained the second and last opposition and follow-up of the third strike for the Provost fo.40
It follows the explanation, guard and stance of the fourth strike which is a high renvers, following the program of this sword alone, for the Lieutenant and Provost and of all that they should do fo.40
It follows also the reason for/of the illustration and the stance for the defending Provost fo.41
Hereafter will be shown and explained the fourth strike of this sword alone, which is a high renvers, being enumerated by the attacking Lieutenant against the defending Provost fo.41
Also after is shown the defence of the fourth strike for the defending Provost fo.42
It follows the first opposition and follow-up of the fourth strike for the attacking Lieutenant against the defending Provost fo.42
Hereafter is show the defence of the first opposition and follow-up of the fourth strike for the Provost against the Lieutenant fo.43
It follows hereafter the second and last opposition and follow-up of the fourth strike, which is a high renvers, and will be also now on the left foot for this opposition, for the attacking Lieutenant and defended also by this current Provost fo.43
After having explained the second opposition, by the attacking Lieutenant, it remains to treat of and explain this second opposition for the defending Provost fo.44
It follows the stance and guard for the attacking Lieutenant and for the defending Provost in order to execute and throw a thrust from above for the fifth strike fo.44
Hereafter is explained the guard and stance for the following Provost in order to defend himself from the fifth strike thrust, thrown hereafter by the Lieutenant fo.45
It follows the fifth strike, which is a thrust from above on the right side[5] following the program of this sword alone for the attacking Lieutenant against the defending Provost fo.45
It follows the defence of the fifth strike which is a thrust from above, relating to [participant] the high maindroit, for the defending Provost against the attacking Lieutenant fo.46
It follows the first opposition and follow-up of the fifth strike, which is a thrust from above, thrown by the attacking Lieutenant against the defending Provost, thus[6] fo.46
Hereafter will be explained the defence of this first opposition and follow-up of the fifth strike for the Provost against the attacking Lieutenant fo.47
It follows the second opposition and follow-up of the fifth strike of this sword alone, which is a thrust from above, for the attacking Lieutenant and for the for defending Provost fo.47
Hereafter will be explained the teaching [tuition] and defence of the second opposition of the

---

4. *suivant l'order dessusdits lieux propres*

5. *maindroit*

6. *que voicy*

Table of this Tract on the Sword Alone

fifth strike, which must guard the following Provost against the Lieutenant   fo.48
here the guard and stance for the Lieutenant and Provost for the sixth strike thrust, being enumerated in the sixth proper place/item on the defender   fo.48
It follows the explanation of the guard and stance for the Provost in order to prepare himself to defend against the thrust from above   fo.49
It follows the sixth and last strike and item of this sword alone, being enumerated, which is a thrust from above on the left side (renvers), thrown by the attacking Lieutenant against the defending Provost   fo.49
After having treated of the sixth strike of this sword alone for the attacking Lieutenant, it remains to treat also of the defence of it for the defending Provost   fo.50
It follows the first opposition and follow-up of the sixth and last strike, being enumerated which is a thrust from above for the attacking Lieutenant and defended by the Provost, here
Hereafter is the defence of this first opposition and follow-up of the sixth strike for the Provost   fo.50 fo.51
Here is the second and last opposition and follow-up of the sixth strike   fo.51
The defence of this second and last opposition and follow-up of the sixth and last strike of this sword alone   fo.52
Here is shown the guard and stance in order to do two good and subtle strikes in the form of the triangle and quadrangle for the attacking Lieutenant against the defending Provost   fo.52
It follows the explanation of the triangle for the defending Provost   fo.53
It follows what he should do in order to execute a very good[7] and subtle strike   fo.53
It follows what the Provost must do to defend from the thrust   fo.54
And for the first opposition and follow-up of the triangle   fo.54
It follows the defence of the first opposition and follow-up for the Provost   fo.55
It follows the second opposition and follow-up which is a high maindroit   fo.55
Explanation, guard and stance for the defending Provost   fo.57
The first strike and follow-up of the quadrangle for the Lieutenant and Provost   fo.57
It follows how the Provost should defend himself from this strike   fo.58
The first opposition and follow-up of the quadrangle for the Lieutenant and Provost   fo.58
It follows the defence of this first opposition of the quadrangle for the defending Provost against the attacking Lieutenant   fo.59
It follows the achieving of the quadrangle, which is on the right side[8] or thrust from above, thrown by the Lieutenant against the Provost   fo.59
It follows the defence and achievement of the strike, with its two follow-ups, in the manner of the quadrangle, for the defending Provost against the attacking Lieutenant   fo.60
Hereafter is shown and explained the outline and stance of the attacking Lieutenant in order to show how to do[9] the first hold against the Provost   fo.60
It follows the guard and stance for the Provost   fo.61
In these two illustrations following …   fo.61
It follows the teaching [tuition] and defence of the first strike for the Provost   fo.62
The first strike, thrown on the maindroit or thrust from above   fo.62
Hereafter will be shown and explained how the Provost can and must make the first hold against the Lieutenant   fo.63

---

7. *un fort bon*
8. *maindroit*
9. *monstrer a faire*

The first hold shown by the Lieutenant	fo.63
It follows the first hold and the explanation of it for the following Provost against the Lieutenant	fo.64
A hold should make a counter-hold, as is here shown by the Lieutenant to the Provost	fo.64
It follows the counter-hold for the Provost against the attacking Lieutenant	fo.65
It follows a counter-hold, shown here above, by the Lieutenant and executed by the Provost	
It follows a very good counter-hold executed for the Lieutenant against the Provost	fo.65
The stance and guard for the second hold for the Lieutenant against the Provost	fo.66 fo.66
After having treated here above of the guard and stance of the Lieutenant, it remains to treat on the guard and stance for the Provost	fo.67
The second hold for the Lieutenant demonstrator against the Provost defender	fo.67
It follows that which the Provost must do for the second hold against the Lieutenant	fo.68
The second hold is shown by the author to the Lieutenant and executed by him against the Provost with the aim that he can do it to another	fo.68
Hereafter will be shown by illustrations and text …	fo.69
This second hold shown and executed by the Lieutenant	fo.69
It follows the demonstration of what the Provost must do in order to remove the sword from the Lieutenant	fo.70
It follows the guard and stance in order to do the third hold for the Lieutenant against the Provost	fo.70
Hereafter is shown the guard and stance for the Provost	fo.71
It follows the first strike in order to make and show the first hold for the Lieutenant and Provost	fo.71
It follows the defence of the second strike	fo.72
The third hold shown and executed by this Lieutenant against the Provost so that the Provost can do it to him and can do it in the future and by consequence afterwards (do it) to any other	
It follows that which the Provost should do, the Lieutenant showing him how to do it	fo.72
The third strike shown here-above by the Lieutenant to the Provost and is here executed by the Provost, it seems[10]	fo.73 fo.73
It follows hereafter what the Provost must do in order to execute the third hold against the Lieutenant	fo.74
The stance and guard of the fourth and last hold for the attacking Lieutenant against the defending Provost	fo.74
It will be hereafter shown the guard and stance in order to defend a strike, which will a maindroit or thrust from above thrown by the Lieutenant against the Provost in order to do the fourth hold	fo.75
A *maindroit* or thrust from above by the Lieutenant and defended by the Provost which should be repeated by the Lieutenant in order to execute the fourth hold against the Provost	fo.75
The means of the Provost defending himself from the above-mentioned maindroit	fo.76
The fourth hold shown by the attacking Lieutenant to the defending Provost, as will be clearly shown and hereafter explained in writing	fo.76

It follows that which the Provost can little do, no knowing any counter-hold yet in all holds there is a counter-hold which he cannot do: but hereafter he will make it by means of[11] the

---

10. *l'appert*.

11. *moyenent*

information[12] the Lieutenant has given him fo.77
The fourth and last hold, executed by the defending Provost against the Lieutenant, his teacher,[13] as here shown by these illustrations, showing him that which was done above fo.77
It follows the execution of this fourth and last hold of this sword alone for the Provost against the Lieutenant, his teacher fo.78
Guard and stance in order to make and execute the subtleties of this sword alone, as much for the attacking Lieutenant as for the defending Provost fo.78
It follows the explanation, guard and stance for the Provost fo.79
The first strike which is a low *maindroit* thrown by the Lieutenant, which serves to test in order to determine[14] ignorance or knowledge, against the Provost fo.79
It follows the defence of this strike for the Provost fo.80
Guard and stance for the Lieutenant and Provost in order for the Lieutenant to show the Provost how he should do (it) henceforth and not as he did in the previous strike fo.80
It follows the text in order to know how to do the Provost's stance and guard in order to execute the said subtlety by the Lieutenant, showing it to the Provost, as will be seen hereafter in the next strike fo.81
The first strike of this subtlety, which is on the first strike of sword alone here shown, by the Lieutenant and executed by the Provost fo.81
It follows all that the Provost should do in order to defend himself and attack at the same time from the the low maindroit to the knee thrown by the Lieutenant against the Provost fo.82
The guard and low stance in order to execute and do the second strike of the subtleties which is a low renvers being on the right foot which will serve to test in order to determine[15] ignorance or knowledge, as much for the attacking Lieutenant as for the defending Provost fo.82
It follows the guard and stance for the Provost and the explanation of it. fo.83
The second strike, which is a low renvers which will serve to test, for better doing and executing the second subtlety for the Lieutenant against the Provost fo.83
It follows that which the Provost does in order to defend from this low renvers thrown by the Lieutenant fo.84
The second strike which is a low renvers on the arm of the Provost thrown and executed by the following Lieutenant against the Provost, showing that he can do such, and not to beat away the sword as he did here-above in the next[16] illustrations fo.84
It follows that which the Provost did fo.85
Another very strong and subtle strike for the Lieutenant against the Provost allowing[17] the backhand on the elbow and to throw a thrust to the belly as is shown here fo.85
It follows what which the Provost must do for the last strike of this sword alone fo.86
It follows a treatise on the use[18] and certain points required to know in the game of tennis[19] for all those who love it composed by the author inasmuch as it required the same stance and knowing the same strikes as swordsmanship [armes] fo.87

12. *l'intelligence*
13. *demonstrateur*
14. *rapporter*
15. *espion pour rapporter*
16. previous?
17. *laissant*
18. *l'exercice*
19. *ieu de la paulme*

Well is it true that one should remove one of the strikes, which is the thrust and only two of them will remain which are ... fo.87

Hereafter will be explained the points which are most necessary[20] in this game and practice [exercise] of tennis which should be well observed fo.88

The third point needed and should be well kept that when on will be inside[21] the game of tennis having one other racket by which one wants to help oneself[22] fo.88

End of the Table

---

20. *fort necessaires*
21. *dedans*
22. *que celle dequoy on se veut aider*

Royal Privilege

Charles, by the grace of god, King of France. To our friends and loyal subjects, those holding our courts of Parliament, Bailiffs, Seneschals, Provosts and their Lieutenants and to all our justices and officers and to each of them, as appropriate,[1] greetings and affection. Our dear and well loved Henry de Sainct-Didier, esquire, gentleman of Provence, has given us to understand that he has composed certain books, which he has dedicated to us, on the the manner of using arms, including the sword alone, sword and dagger, sword and cape, sword and rondelle, sword and targe, sword and buckler, two-handed sword, two swords, and dagger alone, written with art, order and practice, with the means to defend oneself and attack at the same time, with the strikes one can throw, whether attacking or defending, very useful and notable for the guidance of the young, these and similarly all those that he will write about feats of arms, [which] he willingly would like to print and bring into the light. However, being something that he can only do with great cost and expense, he fears that after having out laid the costs, any printers or booksellers or others will greatly disadvantage and injure him[2] by re-printing it, if he has not our permission and special privilege. To this end, we having been humbly begged and beseeched, wanting [to give] him on this power of our letter these necessities, we, in this cause, desire, being that it will be possible, to treat favourably all persons of good knowledge in the training and advancement of things useful and profitable to the public so that everyone may more willingly apply themselves to do the same, we have permitted and granted it to Sainct-Didier. We permit and grant by this present instrument, which could and may be to him open to do by such printing as will seem good to him, the books here above mentioned, and all of them which may be by him composed on the same subject. And to that end, he or those printers who have been charged by him to do this, having the means to recompense them the costs as will be appropriate to doing for this, we have forbidden and protected. We forbid and refuse all other booksellers and printers in this our kingdom, lands and estates under our obedience during the time and term of ten years following from the day and date that these books were printed, they will neither print nor make to be printed, neither big nor small or in any other form as may be, nor sell the above-mentioned books which have been printed by others and not by him or those who have been charged by Sainct-Didier on

1. *si comme à luy appartiendra*
2. lit: do not make it to his great detriment and injury

penalty of fixed fine[3] and of confiscation and loss of all the books. So we want and command you, we charge and impose by these letters, and to each of you in his own right,[4] as appropriate[5], that according to and following our permissions to grant and desire, to make and cause to be made[6] express interdictions and protections from us on the above-mentioned penalties and others which you will seek to impose on all printers and booksellers situated in your districts and jurisdictions that hereafter they – any of them – other than those who will be charged and expressly commissioned by Sainct-Didier in order to print or cause to be printed or expose them for sale during the period of ten years these above-mentioned books. And if after making the injunctions you find any contravening these, proceed against them both by sentencing with the said penalties as well as those you seek to be done according to the circumstances of the case, such is our pleasure and because of the content of these letters they apply in several and diverse places. We want that a *vidimus*[7] on this made under the royal seal or examined by one of our notaries and secretaries made or adjusted to match this present original and that putting by brief or extract the contents of this at the start of the books they may be held to be duly authorised[8] to all above-mentioned booksellers and libraries as appropriate.

Given in Paris on the 23rd day of January in the year of grace 1573 and third of our reign, thus signed by the king and sealed on a simple tail of yellow wax.

3. *peine arbitraire*
4. *en droit soy*
5. lit: as like will belong to him
6. *faites faire*
7. a medieval French legal formula "we have seen" used for document attestation
8. *deuement signifiees*

PART II

Images from the Text

Portrait of King Charles IX of France

Portrait of Henry de Sainct-Didier

Images 1 and 2, 3 and 4

Images 5 and 6, 7 and 8

Images from the Main Text   111

Images 9 and 10, 11 and 12

Images 13 and 14, 15 and 16

Images from the Main Text   113

Images 17 and 18, 19 and 20

Images 21 and 22, 23 and 24

Images 25 and 26, 27 and 28

Images 29 and 30, 31 and 32

Images from the Main Text

Images 33 and 34, 35 and 36

118 Secrets of the Sword Alone

Images 37 and 38, 39 and 40

Images 41 and 42, 43 and 44

Images 45 and 46, 47 and 48

Images 49 and 50, 51 and 52

Images 53 and 54, 55 and 56

Images from the Main Text 123

Images 57 and 58, 59 and 60

Images 61 and 62, 63 and 64

Images 65 and 66, 67 and 68

Images 69 and 70, 71 and 72

Images from the Main Text

Images 73 and 74, 75 and 76

Images 77 and 78, 79 and 80

Images from the Main Text 129

Images 81 and 82, 83 and 84

Images 85 and 86, 87 and 88

Images from the Main Text 131

Images 89 and 90, 91 and 92

132 Secrets of the Sword Alone

Images 93 and 94, 95 and 96

Images 97 and 98, 99 and 100

Images 101 and 102, 103 and 104

Images from the Main Text 135

Images 105 and 106, 107 and 108

Images 109 and 110, 111 and 112

Images from the Main Text

Images 113 and 114, 115 and 116

Images 117 and 118, 119 and 120

Images from the Main Text   139

Images 121 and 122, 123 and 124

Images 125 and 126, 127 and 128

www.ingramcontent.com/pod-product-compliance
Lightning Source LLC
Chambersburg PA
CBHW020744100426
42735CB00037B/452